A Christian View of Origins

Donald England

BAKER BOOK HOUSE
Grand Rapids, Michigan

Figures 12, 13, and the right hand column of Figure 22 from
Scientific American are used with permission of W. H. Freeman
Company. Quotations from *Biochemistry* by A. L. Lehninger are
used with permission of Worth Publishing Company.

THE UNIVERSITY CHRISTIAN
STUDENT CENTER ANNUAL LECTURESHIP

The University Christian Student Center at the University of Mississippi is a private foundation which exists to provide fellowship and guidance in a home away from home atmosphere for university students during their academic careers. While maintaining a dormitory and a fellowship hall adjacent to the university campus, the Center by worship activities, by instruction in Biblical subjects, and by social activities seeks to supplement the classroom educational experiences of the student and to make a contribution toward the enrichment of his life.

As a portion of its regular program, the Center sponsors an annual lectureship on "Christian Faith in the Contemporary World" in which a competent Christian lecturer is invited to present a series of lectures on a topic concerning faith that vitally confronts the student during the course of his education. The aim is to present the claims of faith not only as a valid alternative to the secularism which characterizes much of our society, but also as intellectually challenging, and as offering the solution to many of the ills of the current age.

ACKNOWLEDGMENTS

The author wishes to express his appreciation to the Board of Directors and Mr. James Taylor of the University Christian Student Center for inviting me to present the 1971 fall lecture series on the contents of this text. The Christian students of Ole Miss are deserving of commendation for the respectful manner in which they received the lectures.

Dr. Neal Pryor and Dr. J. D. Bales of Harding College and Dr. Douglas Shields of Ole Miss read portions of the rough manuscript while it was in preparation. However, these gentlemen should not be held responsible for any shortcoming inherent in the text. My colleague and active catalyst, Dr. W. D. Williams, deserves a special note of appreciation as do my other colleagues in the science division at Harding College. My wife, Lynn, and secretary, Mary Groves, typed the manuscript.

CONTENTS

LIST OF FIGURES

LIST OF TABLES

CHAPTER 1

MAN'S CONCEPTS CONCERNING ORIGINS

The Problem Is Philosophical in Nature

Basically, the problem of origins has its roots in philosophy. As one inquires as to his ultimate origin or even the "stuff" of which he is made, his thought must eventually pass beyond the realm of what is experimentally observable into the realms of metaphysics, theology, and philosophy. This is true because the origin of the universe and the origin of life were not observable events nor were they events that can be repeated at will in the laboratory for scientific observation and study. However, this book is no text on philosophy, although much of what is said has philosophical overtones. Perhaps the greatest fault of most scientific statements made in our time is that philosophical implications are generally ignored. If any scientist is limited by his philosophical predisposition or presupposition to mechanistic explanations alone, then the theological alternative is, of course, eliminated. The burden of this text is to show that it is not reasonable to ignore the theological alternative in respect to the problem of origins.

Our Search for Knowledge on the Subject of Origins

Our search for knowledge, in general, is limited to four sources. These are (a) personal intuition, (b) rationalism as was exploited by the ancient Greeks, (c) empiricism, which is the scientific approach, and (d) revelation from a divine source. An adequate comparison of the limitations, scope, and reliability of each of these methods is beyond the scope of this text.

a. Intuition

It should be sufficient to say that personal intuition can tell us nothing of our origin nor of the origin of the universe, for what one may feel about his origin will have little or no bearing on the ultimate truth of the matter. Intuition is a subjective method that normally leads to private rather than

13

public knowledge. Intuitive knowledge cannot normally be rationally analyzed or tested by an observer. One possible exception to this is that mathematical or otherwise scientific concepts which arise intuitively can sometimes be checked experimentally.[1] Intuitive knowledge of this sort may be made public. For example, in 1926 E. Schrodinger published a mathematical equation that was to revolutionize scientific thought relative to atomic structure. When pressed by his contemporaries to show a scientific reason for the validity of his equation, he could not. However, the equation works experimentally and has served as a fairly reliable predictive tool in scientific research since 1926. It is one of the most outstanding examples of how mathematical intuition of one genius has led to public knowledge, though not knowledge in the sense of absolute truth.

b. Rationalism

Rationalism makes use of the reasoning activities of the mind for formulating concepts and deriving knowledge. It is sometimes called the "arm-chair" method and was used extensively by the ancient Greeks. Thales of Miletus was the first philosopher to use the method of rationalism in an effort to answer the question, "How, and of what, is the world made?"[2] He concluded that the primal substance of matter was water. Heraclitus, and later Empedocles, said that it was earth, fire, air, and water. Democritus was more nearly accurate than his predecessors in that he supposed the primal substance to be atoms.

René Descartes (1596-1650) and Immanuel Kant (1724-1804) more recently were notable advocates of rationalism. Descartes used this method to the exclusion of all other methods, and it caused him to doubt everything but his own existence. He was sure of only one thing: there was someone who was doubting. He, therefore, formulated the conclusion that is closely associated with his name, "I think, therefore I am." Rationalism alone is clearly of limited value as a means of obtaining reliable knowledge. Indeed, it is likely to be no more successful for us than it was for the ancient Greeks as pertaining to the problem of our origin.

c. The Scientific Empirical Approach

We are then left with two alternatives: the scientific empirical approach and divine revelation. It is apparent that science, generally speaking, and

1. R. L. Wilder, "The Role of Intuition," *Science,* 5 May 1967, p. 605.
2. G. Feinberg, "Ordinary Matter," *Scientific American,* May 1967, p. 126.

traditional interpretations of Biblical revelation are very much in conflict as to the question of the origin of life on earth. Furthermore, we are deceiving ourselves if we say that this conflict is apparent rather than real.

Our search for knowledge through scientific empirical methods is illustrated schematically in Figure 1. With the aid of human senses and

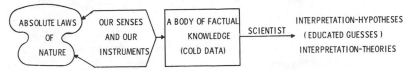

Fig. 1.   The empirical (scientific) approach to a discovery of knowledge

scientific instruments, such as balances and spectrophotometers, the scientist probes into the absolute, unchanging laws of nature. This probing results in the formation of a body of factual knowledge, or cold, hard data. The scientist then formulates "educated guesses" or hypotheses in an attempt to conceptualize by way of a mental model the meaning of his data. A sophistication of the hypotheses generally results in their being called theories; and, if the theory stands the test of time and rigorous experimentation, it may be regarded as a scientific law. However, scientific laws are merely statements that are derived from man's experimentation and intellect; they are not to be equated with the absolute laws of nature, for they are only approximate interpretations of these laws. Our verbal and even mathematical statements of scientific laws change as scientific thought progresses; however, God's absolute laws of nature do not change. It is unfortunate that man's formulation of scientific laws is often equated with God's created laws of nature.

All knowledge derived by way of the scientific process is relative to a point of reference. True objectivity in science is impossible; it is an illusion. The scientist does not discover or elucidate absolutes. In fact, should a scientist discover an absolute he would not know what to do with it because the scientist can only work with what can be tested and measured, and absolutes cannot be tested or measured.

It is appropriate to emphasize that in the final analysis all scientific knowledge is predicated on faith. The following represent four areas of scientific faith:

1. The scientist has faith in the very reality of the material world. This may sound ridiculous at first, but try to convince a nonbeliever

sometime that you are more than just an illusion or perhaps a figment of his imagination. Philosophically speaking, the proof is impossible. Therefore, you accept by faith the fact of your own reality.

2. The scientist has faith in the reliability of his senses, his instruments, and the accuracy of the calibration of his instruments.

3. The scientist has faith in the regularity, consistency, uniformity, and orderliness of nature. Incidentally, the Christian who attributes nature to the creation of God should accept this presupposition of the scientist because God Himself is consistent.

4. The scientist has faith in his ability to comprehend nature, but he does not expect to be able to do this perfectly. Why should we seek for an understanding of the cause of cancer if we do not expect to find an answer? The scientist seeks with an expectation of understanding. Yet all prior scientific exploration has consistently revealed that nature cannot be perfectly comprehended. We evidently stand little chance of ever perceiving even the edge of our awesome universe. To the other extreme, the utter complexity of a living cell, like nuclear and atomic structure, seems to us now incomprehensible.

d. Divine Revelation

Revelation from an authority is a dogmatic method (this does not make it any less valuable) and leads to public knowledge. This is the most common of all methods used in obtaining knowledge, and is the method used in classroom teaching. It is impossible for a student to learn today, for example, by experimentation, the knowledge that is available on the atomic theory. The method is used as we read our newspapers or listen to a play-by-play description of a football game over the radio. We use this method as other people relate to us details of events we ourselves did not witness.

Three factors determine the reliability of revelation as a source of knowledge. First is the knowledge of our authoritative source; second is the ability of this authority to accurately relate information to us; and third is our ability to comprehend what is revealed to us. In our case, God, or the infinite of the universe, is our authority. We cannot limit God in His ability either to know perfectly or to perfectly transmit that knowledge to humanity. To limit Him in either of these respects is to deny Him the quality of the infinite, which is to deny Him existence. The great limiting factor is the mind of finite man. Perhaps the greatest single factor in our inability to understand Biblical revelation where it bears on origins is our inherent inability to comprehend fully those very things our creator has revealed to us. This is not to say that all of Biblical revelation is incomprehensible.

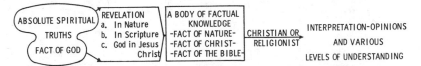

Fig. 2.   Divine revelation as a source of knowledge

Our search for knowledge through Biblical revelation is illustrated in Figure 2. Man cannot probe for spiritual truths independently of divine revelation as the scientist probes for an understanding of the behavior of nature. Anything we are to learn about the spiritual world and the nature of God must come to us through some sort of revelation. An outpouring of divine revelation has come to us through three avenues: (1) nature, which is the handiwork of God (Ps. 19:1; Rom. 1:19, 20); (2) the inspiration of Scripture (II Tim. 3:16); and (3) the revelation of God in the historical person Jesus Christ (John 1:1, 14). These three revelatory sources constitute a body of factual knowledge which we accept as true through faith. This faith is substantiated by historical evidence. As a Christian or religionist exposes himself to this body of knowledge, there is produced within him various levels of understanding regarding absolute spiritual truths and the nature of God. However, it is utterly presumptuous, as well as the height of conceit, for one to suppose that he comprehends fully the intimacy of spiritual things and the nature of God. However, we may rest fully assured that through faith we can know spiritual truths sufficiently to meet our needs.

Brief consideration will now be given to some of the aspects of the philosophical nature of the problem of origins.

Materialism

Materialism is a branch of philosophy that deals with the nature and number of ultimate principles to be assumed in order to explain the universe. Dualism is the philosophical approach which claims that there are two ultimate principles which are necessary to account for the whole of reality: mind (spirit) and matter. Monism, on the other hand, says that

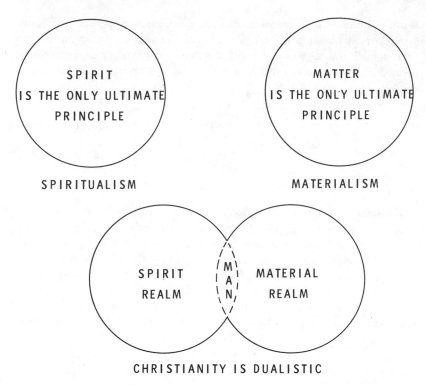

Fig. 3. *Philosophical systems of spiritualism, materialism, and
dualism (Christianity)*

there is only one ultimate principle: it is either mind (spiritualism) or
matter (materialism). Either of these extremes is inconsistent with Christian philosophy, which is, of course, dualistic. Man's nature, for example,
is both material and spiritual. His physical body consists principally of the
elements carbon, oxygen, hydrogen, and nitrogen; and his body will
ultimately decay to these elements. But man is more than this: he is also a
spiritual being, having been created in the spiritual image of God.

Strict materialism is necessarily atheistic. Materialism affirms that there
is no God and that matter is the only eternal entity, or else matter created
itself by evolving into existence from perfect nothingness. The latter case
is to say that matter embodies the attributes of a creator. This, to say the
least, does not appeal to reason.

Mechanistic Materialism

Mechanistic materialism is a deterministic system which maintains that living systems are simply automata; that is, all life principles and life's origin can ultimately be reduced to the molecular interaction of matter in accordance with the laws of physics and chemistry. The cause-and-effect assumption is taken to be operative in human behavior just as in physics. For example, according to mechanistic materialism, the origin of all consciousness is supposed to lie in the molecular activity within brain cells alone. There is, therefore, ultimately no right or wrong according to this philosophy. This of course excludes the possibility of the existence of a human will, a conclusion which is obviously anti-Christian. Mechanistic materialism is not without its competent criticism, as is evidenced by the recent writings of the eminent British science philosopher, M. Polanyi, M.D., Ph.D. For example, this widely recognized author and lecturer claims that "to speak of life as something to be explained by the laws of physics and chemistry is strictly speaking absurd, for physical and chemical processes do not determine by themselves any finite system."[3] Furthermore, Polanyi states, "When I say that life transcends physics and chemistry, I mean that biology cannot explain life in our age by the current workings of physical and chemical laws."[4]

The Christian may safely invoke mechanistic explanations for the phenomena of nature. It is only when mechanism is allied with the philosophy of materialism that mechanism comes in conflict with Christian thought, for materialism maintains that there is no such thing as Spirit. For example, the Christian interprets weather phenomena by use of such mechanistic terms as high pressures, low pressures, and temperature inversions; but, in the final analysis, he attributes these phenomena to laws of nature which God created. The mechanistic materialist, on the other hand, may give exactly the same mechanistic interpretation to the weather phenomena; but he attributes the high pressures, low pressures, and temperature inversions, not to laws of nature created by God, but to forces totally inherent within matter itself. The Christian is free to interpret all phenomena of nature mechanistically—in fact, the Christian who is

3. M. Polanyi, "Life Transcending Physics and Chemistry," *Chemical and Engineering News*, 21 August 1967, p. 62.
4. Polanyi, p. 54.

also a scientist has no alternative—but all the while he advocates that there is Spirit transcending and maintaining the material world.

The First and Crucial Presupposition

Let us now look at the first and crucial presupposition bearing on the problem of origins. A presupposition is merely a stated assumption which by its inherent nature cannot be verified by demonstration or be ultimately proved. Evidence may be accumulated in support or denial of the presupposition, but it cannot be absolutely or ultimately demonstrated. The presupposition must be accepted as true or rejected as false on faith. Our basic presupposition then is our starting point; and in regard to the problem of origins, our first presupposition is most crucial.

The first presupposition of mechanistic materialism is: *the only eternal principle is matter;* or else: *matter is its own creator.* Either of these presuppositions is the very antithesis of the first presupposition of the Christian, which is: *the only eternal principle is Spirit.*

It is interesting that the first statement of the Book of Genesis announces the first presupposition of Christianity: "In the beginning God. . . ." Throughout the Bible it is affirmed that God, YAHWEH, is the creator of all things living and nonliving. "The heavens are telling the glory of God; and the firmament proclaims his handiwork," sings the psalmist David, but nowhere in all the Bible is a systematic, ultimate proof of God's being undertaken. God's existence is left to the province of faith, and "by faith we understand that the world was created by the word of God, so that what is seen was made out of things which do not appear" (Heb. 11:3). If any doubt remains as to a Biblical proof of the existence of God, then read carefully Hebrews 11:6: "For whoever would draw near to God must believe that he exists and that he rewards those who seek him."

It is significant that the writer of Hebrews did not say that we know or demonstrate that God exists. Empirically based knowledge and faith are mutually exclusive; for where there is knowledge, faith is pushed aside. If this is disturbing, it is perhaps because of an improper evaluation of the scope and meaning of faith. Faith makes real in our lives those things which we cannot personally see or otherwise directly experience with our senses. Faith gives meaning, substance, and conviction to our lives (Heb. 11:1). The Christian walks by faith and not by sight. He therefore acknowledges that he cannot demonstrate in an absolute or ultimate sense that his basic presupposition that *the only eternal principle is Spirit* is correct. Furthermore, he feels no sense of obligation to do so. Neither does the materialist feel an obligation to demonstrate in an absolute sense that his basic presupposition that *the only eternal principle is matter* is correct. However, we have now reached an impasse. Both antithetical presuppositions cannot possibly be true; one is false. The following evidence to be presented in this text weighs strongly in favor of the Christian presupposition, though it is contended that scientific facts, figures, and reasoning do not prove God's existence nor His methods of working in and through nature. Findings in science may tend to substantiate our faith but science per se does not prove God.

It may seem strange to us at first, but we should realize that *within the framework of the materialistic presupposition* it is reasonable that a **spontaneous generation of life*** and its subsequent evolution occurred—because *here we are*. However, we must also realize that *within the framework of the theistic presupposition* it does not necessarily follow that the spontaneous generation of life and its subsequent evolution occurred.

Beginning with chapter 2 we will explore problems and research bearing on a materialistic approach to the origin of life. Only in this way can the proper status of divine revelation on the subject of origins be recognized and appreciated. However, inasmuch as the earth's **primordial** (primitive or original) state determined the formation and availability of **bio-organic** compounds from which life could spontaneously arise and evolve, it is felt that a brief survey of hypotheses advanced to explain the nature of the universe and the origin of our solar system would be in order.

COSMOLOGICAL ORIGINS

Introduction: The Vastness of the Universe

When I look at thy heavens, the work of thy fingers,
the moon and the stars which thou hast established;
what is man that thou art mindful of him,
and the son of man that thou dost care for him? (Ps. 8:3, 4).

Relatively speaking, the earth is a tiny speck moving through space at a speed of 18 miles per second. Its mass is 6,000,000,000,000,000,000,000 tons; yet our sun has a mass 330,000 times as great. Our solar system consists of our sun and nine planets, with the sun making up 99.8 percent of the total mass of the solar system. The sun has a diameter of 864,000

---

*All bold-faced words in textual matter are defined or illustrated in the glossary.

miles. If we imagine the sun reduced to the size of a basketball, the earth in proportion would be the size of a BB shot 109 feet from the sun, Jupiter would be the size of a ping-pong ball 570 feet from the sun, Pluto would be smaller than a BB shot 4,300 feet from the sun, and the distance to the nearest known star would be 5,700 miles.[5]

Think of our earth as being the size of a pinhead. In proportion, the sun would be a sphere 6 inches in diameter 50 feet away; Jupiter, the largest planet in our solar system, would be one-half inch in diameter 250 feet from the sun; and Alpha Centauri, our nearest star neighbor, would be another 6-inch sphere 2,000 miles away![6]

Traveling at the speed of light of 186,000 miles per second, a person could circle the earth 410 times in one minute at an altitude of 50 miles. At the same speed it would take light one year to travel 6 million million miles (one light year), or four and one-half years to reach our sun's nearest star neighbor. These two stars are a part of a cluster of stars within our galaxy (Fig. 4), which is spiral shaped, having a thickness of 10,000-15,000 light years at the center or hub of the spiral. Our solar system is about 30,000 light years from the center of the spiral and, at this point, the

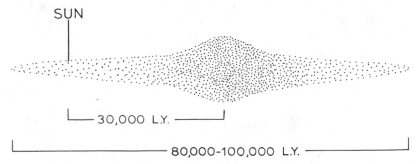

Fig. 4.   A cross sectional drawing of our galaxy

galaxy has a thickness of about 1,000 light years. Its overall diameter is about 80,000-100,000 light years. All attempts to conceptualize these vast numbers are met with futility. Astronomers tell us that if our galaxy were reduced to the size of the earth (8,000 miles in diameter), then on this scale our sun would be an invisible speck of dust 0.00008 inches across. Other suns in this agglomeration of stars would be separated by one-third

5. E. G. Ebbighausen, *Astronomy* (Columbus, Ohio: Charles E. Merrill Books, Inc., 1966), p. 50.
6. M. W. Ovenden, *Life in the Universe* (Garden City, N.Y.: Doubleday and Co., Inc., 1962), pp. 17, 18.

mile and would be other specks of dust of various sizes ranging perhaps from a near invisible 0.008 inches in diameter to a microscopic 0.0000008 inches in diameter.

Were we to board a spaceship and travel at the inconceivable speed of 186,000 miles per second (present spaceships have reached speeds of only about eight miles per second), we would arrive at Alpha Centauri, our nearest star neighbor, in four and one-half years. We would arrive at Sirius in eight and one-half years, Aldebaran in fifty-five years, and Rigel in 543 years. However, we still would not have even so much as left the immediate neighborhood of our own galaxy. In fact, had a person left planet Earth in B.C. 1 and traveled at the rate of present Apollo spaceships, he would be less than two-tenths of one percent of the way toward our nearest star neighbor by the year A.D. 2000. There are perhaps 200 billion (one billion is equal to 1,000 million) stars in our galaxy,[7] and the number of galaxies in the entire universe is also estimated to figure into the billions. Have modern telescopes enabled astronomers to "see" the edge of the universe? No, but it seems rather that astronomers have nearly reached the limits of their observations without hope of ever "seeing" the outer edge of the universe.

Our sun is average in size, with some stars having masses one hundred times as great and some having masses one hundred times less. All of earth's energy (except nuclear) comes from the sun. There it originates as matter and is converted into energy during the fusion of hydrogen into helium in keeping with Einstein's equation $E=mc^2$. In this equation m stands for mass, which is expressed in grams; and c stands for the speed of light, expressed in centimeters per second. Calculations based on this equation show that the sun is burning up at the rate of about 5 million tons per second but that it will continue to burn at its present intensity for billions of years. The earth receives only a minute portion of the energy produced by the sun; the remainder simply escapes into space. In one second the sun emits more energy than the entire human species has consumed through its entire history.

Two of Man's Concepts of the Universe

a. Geocentric or Ptolemaic

Man has not always had the same world view as he has today. In fact, twentieth century man has a plurality of world views. There exists, to this day, in spite of American and Russian space efforts, an active organization

7. O. Struve, *The Universe* (Cambridge, Mass.: The M. I. T. Press, 1962), p. 81.

known as the Flat Earth Society. It is, therefore, not surprising that over the centuries mankind has had many different views of cosmology.

The Ptolemaic concept of the universe (Fig. 5) is primitive and was due mainly to the work of Ptolemy, about A.D. 150. The concept maintained that the earth was the center of the universe and that the planets, sun, and

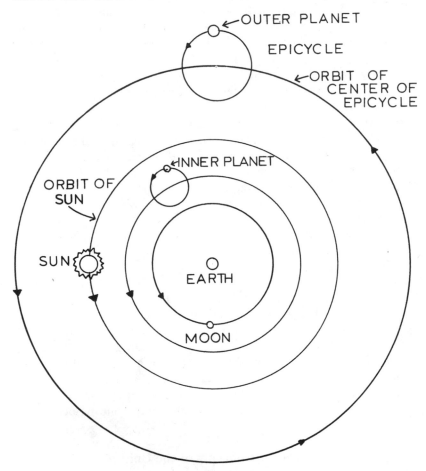

Fig. 5. The Ptolemaic view of the solar system

stars revolved around the earth. The precise details of this **geocentric** system depended on the extent of sophistication of the theory, but it necessitated a complete revolution of the background of stars around the earth each twenty-four hours. The system was aesthetically pleasing inasmuch as it made the earth the center of the universe. However, unreasonable assumptions had to be made to explain precise details of planetary motion until it became apparent that the Ptolemaic system had to give way to another concept.

b. Heliocentric or Copernican

The Copernican concept of the universe (Fig. 6), with few modifications, is the one presently accepted and is mainly due to the work of the Polish astronomer Nicholas Copernicus (1473-1543). This concept places the sun at the center of the solar system and has the planets revolving

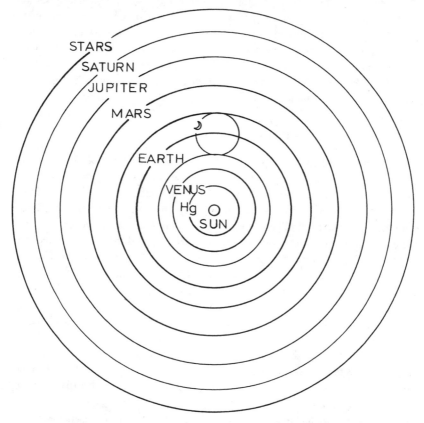

Fig. 6. The Copernican view of the solar system (Hg=Mercury)

around it. The confirmation of this concept is attributed to Galileo's careful observations of Jupiter's moons, which observations were based on the preceding work of Tycho Brahe (1546-1601) of Sweden and his student Johaunes Kepler (1571-1630). Galileo's studies, in turn, served as a basis for Newton's laws of motion and the determination of the speed of light. History gives evidence that the supplanting of the Ptolemaic with the Copernican concept resulted in much theological controversy.

Origin of the Solar System: Introduction

In the discussion to follow we will see that science is incapable of speaking authoritatively regarding the subject of cosmological origins. In particular, we want to note the assumptions and objections to the most notable hypotheses bearing on the problem of the origin of the solar system. Since the solar system is a part of the whole universe, it naturally follows that *if science cannot speak authoritatively regarding the origin of a part of the universe, it certainly cannot speak authoritatively regarding the origin of the whole universe.*

a. The Encounter Hypothesis

The encounter hypothesis assumes the prior existence of the sun and proposes that another star passed near our sun, causing a great tidal wave of sun material to escape into space. The sun material broke into fragments of hot gases which were trapped by the sun's gravitational field, cooled and condensed. These fragments became planets. However, calculations indicate that the gaseous sun material would have continued to expand into space rather than cooling and condensing into planets. Even if it had cooled and condensed, the planets Neptune and Pluto are too far from our sun to be accounted for by this hypothesis. Furthermore, the eminent astronomer Jeans calculated that the probability of such a collision of stars is on the average of once in 600,000 billions of years, which is many times greater than the most liberal estimates for the total age of the universe.[8] This hypothesis also predicts that the planets should move in elliptical orbits about the sun; whereas, in reality, they move in almost perfectly circular orbits. The encounter hypothesis holds very little favor

8. H. S. Jones, *Life on Other Worlds* (New York: New American Library, n.d.), p. 16.

among modern astronomers, but in years past it held great esteem among cosmologists.

b. The Nebular Hypothesis

The nebular hypothesis assumes the prior existence of a nebula of gaseous material with the shape of a pinwheel and rotating in the manner of a pinwheel. Through the passing of time, a gaseous ring would occasionally break from the rotating mass, condense, and become a planet. It is proposed that the residual central material became our sun. A main objection to this hypothesis is that calculations show that if the hypothesis were correct then the sun should be rotating once every few hours instead of once every twenty-seven days. Consequently, proponents of the hypothesis have had to propose unsatisfying elaborate "breaking mechanisms" to account for the slowing down of the sun's rotation. The predicated rapid revolution of the sun about its axis is easily understood. We have observed than an ice skater revolves faster on her toes as she slowly brings her outstretched arms in close to her body. Likewise a vast, revolving nebula of gaseous sun material should rotate faster and faster as it condenses into a more compact mass. Several variations of the nebular hypothesis have been advanced in efforts to rationalize its several difficulties.

c. The Random-Capture Hypothesis

The random-capture hypothesis assumes the preexistence of the sun and a myriad of small floating bodies in space. The sun's gravitational field is supposed to have captured the material bodies and the planets were formed as the result of the bodies clustering together. The hypothesis has been generally rejected for a number of reasons, one being that the hypothesis predicates that the planets would be revolving about the sun in both directions but they are all traveling in the same direction. One astronomer states, "It is not possible for the sun (or any other star) to capture such an object."[9]

d. The Proto-Planet Hypothesis

The proto-planet hypothesis is the most recent, but not necessarily the best, of the hypotheses relating to the origin of the solar system. The

9. Ebbighausen, p. 71.

hypothesis presupposes the prior existence of a rotating cloud of cool gas and dust in space. The cloud collapsed into a large central mass (later to become the sun) and smaller spherical masses (proto-planets), later to cool and condense into the planets. The main objection here is similar to the objection to the nebular hypothesis; namely, the theory predicates that the sun should be rotating one hundred times faster than it is. Consequently, it again has been necessary to propose elaborate, but unsatisfying, "braking mechanisms" to account for the slower rotation of the sun. Also, this theory predicates that the sum of the masses of the planets should be approximately one-third of the total mass of the sun; whereas, in fact, the total mass of the planets is only approximately one-thousandth the mass of the sun.[10]

In short, none of the hypotheses bearing on the origin of the solar system are complete or satisfying. However, we would not want to deny scientists the right to propose models for the origin of the solar system; for this is the very essence of the scientific approach to problems. We do, however, wish to point out that all hypotheses bearing on the origin of the solar system accept by faith the prior existence of matter from which the solar system was made. Each hypothesis is faced with serious objections. Even if a satisfying hypothesis were forthcoming, it still remains that the origin of the solar system was a prehistorical event. No human observers were present, no observations were recorded, and the process cannot be reproduced by human hands for verification. Let us remember that our solar system is only an infinitesimal portion of the total universe. Our earlier statement is still valid: *If science cannot speak authoritatively regarding the origin of a part of the universe, it certainly cannot speak authoritatively regarding the origin of the whole universe.* Nevertheless, there are scientific hypotheses which attempt to explain the origin of the whole universe. We will now deal briefly with three of the most notable of these hypotheses.

Origin of the Universe: Introduction

Without observations there can be no meaningful hypotheses, theories, or conclusions. Regarding the problem of cosmological origins, Ebbighausen, a University of Oregon astronomer, said, "There is no dearth of models, but there is a scarcity of trustworthy, interpretable observa-

10. R. Jastrow, *Red Giants and White Dwarfs* (New York: Harper and Row Publishers, 1967), p. 63.

tions."[11] In spite of a lack of "trustworthy, interpretable observations," scientists have justifiably felt a sense of obligation to bring forth models or concepts bearing on the origin of the universe. However, since these hypotheses of cosmological origins are but models or concepts based on a scarcity of observations, they are essentially statements of faith and should not be accepted as factual at the expense of other statements of faith regarding the origin of the universe.

a. The Big-Bang Hypothesis

From the astronomical observation that the observable galaxies of the universe appear to be expanding has come the assumption that about ten to twenty billions of years ago all matter of the universe was concentrated in one mass which astronomers call the "primeval atom." About ten billion years ago the matter exploded (the big bang, Fig. 7a), causing the universe to embark on a cosmological era of expansion. From the expanding gases condensed the galaxies, stars, and planets. The theory was expounded and elaborated by Lemaître, Jeans, Eddington and Gamow; and Jeans spoke of "the finger of God agitating the ether."[12] According to the proponents of this hypothesis, all of the elements which make up the earth's crust were formed during the first thirty minutes of the existence of the universe. As to the origin of the primeval atom, scientists are silent.

Concerning the big-bang hypothesis, A. C. B. Lovell, director of the Jodrell Bank Observatory, says:

> But when we inquire what the primeval atom was like, how it disintegrated and by what means and at what time it was created we begin to cross the boundaries of physics into the realms of philosophy and theology. The important thing at that stage is what you and I think about the situation, this beginning of all time and space.[13]

Lovell continues:

> As a scientist I cannot discuss this problem of the creation of the primeval atom because it precedes the moment when I can

11. Ebbighausen, pp. 118, 119.
12. A. C. B. Lovell, *The Individual and the Universe* (New York: Harper & Row, Publishers, 1958), p. 84.
13. Lovell, p. 91.

ever hope to infer from observations the conditions which existed.[14]

In conclusion, it should be noted that the prior existence of primeval matter is assumed. It, therefore, is not a hypothesis of ultimate creation at all.

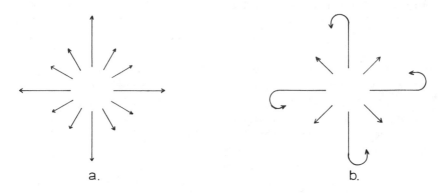

a.   b.

*Fig. 7. A diagrammatic representation of (a) the big-bang hypo-
thesis and (b) the oscillating universe hypothesis*

b. The Oscillating Universe Hypothesis

The oscillating universe concept of the origin of the universe is essentially the same as the big-bang hypothesis, but was brought forth partially in an attempt to avoid the problem of time zero and the question of the source of the original primeval matter. The proponents claim that matter has existed from all eternity and that the universe has gone through an indefinite number of cycles consisting of big bang—expansion—contraction—big bang, and so forth (Fig. 7b). However, reason compels that the process had to start somewhere. If it started, where it started, how it started, and the question of original matter are all answerable only through faith. To deny that creation occurred and that time had a beginning is not only to violate reason, but is to hold in question the evidences of science (radioactivity, first and second laws of thermodynamics, entropy, etc.) that the universe indeed had a moment of creation.

14. Lovell.

c. The Steady-State Hypothesis

The steady-state hypothesis also denies that there has been a moment of creation. It maintains that the universe has basically had the same appearance in the eternal past as it has at present and that it will retain this basic appearance for the eternal future. However, this necessitates that matter is continuously being created to compensate for the overall decrease in space density due to the expansion of the universe. This creation, of course, is not observed directly and is supposed to occur only at the rate of one atom of hydrogen per cubic yard of space per ten billions of years. The theory admittedly violates the law of conservation of matter and energy and has all the earmarks of being highly improbable. Allowing validity to the assumption that the law of conservation of matter and energy is wrong is like allowing a person to divide by zero. It permits virtually any conclusion to be drawn. Since all laboratory experiments have tended to confirm the law of conservation of matter and energy, it would require an unusual amount of faith to cause one to accept the steady-state hypothesis. Also, there remain the same objections to this hypothesis as were seen for the oscillating universe hypothesis regarding the demands of science for a moment of creation and a beginning of measurable time. The concept does not appeal to reason.

d. Special Creation

All observations within science favor a moment of creation and the beginning of measurable time. For example, from a consideration of the first and second laws of thermodynamics, we learn that the total energy content of the universe is constant and that the universe tends toward greater degrees of disorganization. In other words, the universe exhibits the appearance of a clock running down, thus implying that it was once "wound up" or set in motion.

It does not appear reasonable that matter created itself, that it spontaneously sprang into existence from out of nothing, or that it has existed eternally. However, considering all available evidence, it seems reasonable to assume that prior to the existence of matter and prior to the beginning of measurable time, there existed the one eternal spiritual entity, God. It is then not unexpected that His revelation to man declares: "In the beginning God created the heavens and the earth" (Gen. 1:1). God is the eternal first cause; creation is, therefore, supernatural and is beyond experimental verification. Anything we are to know absolutely about creation must be given to us by a special act of revelation from the creator. By revelation we can learn some of the essential features of creation; however, God has chosen to reveal to us none of the material mechanics of the creation event.

It is significant that the astronomer A. C. B. Lovell reached the following conclusion after examining all the present natural attempts to account for the origin of the universe:

> Finally, we shall reach a stage where theories based on our present conceptions of physical laws have nothing further to say. At this point we pass from physics to metaphysics, from astronomy to theology, where the corporate views of science merge into the beliefs of the individual.[15]

Robert Jastrow, director of the Goddard Institute for Space Studies, acknowledges, "science offers no satisfactory answer to one of the most profound questions to occupy the mind of man—the question of the beginning and end."[16] Lincoln Barnett states, "Cosmologists for the most part remain silent on the question of ultimate origins, leaving the issue to the philosophers and theology."[17]

The question arises as to why it is more reasonable to assume that God is the eternal entity as opposed to matter being the eternal entity. Based on our present observations of the behavior of the material world, reason compels that it is irrational that matter could have spontaneously arisen out of a total void of empty nothingness, where only absolute cold prevailed and not even a photon of light raced across the perfect vacuum of space. However, it does not seem unreasonable to presuppose the prior existence of an omnipotent, eternal, spiritual being, God, who was and still is external, supra, and transcendent to the material world and who called it into existence at His own will. Incomprehensible, yes; unreasonable, no. Lovell's observation is, therefore, true that creation preceded the moment when one can ever hope to infer from observations the conditions that existed. Scientific empiricism as a source of final knowledge regarding the origin of the material world is inadequate. Reason and logic, therefore, compel that the position of faith—based on the Biblical revelation that "in the beginning God created the heavens and the earth"—is valid.

15. Lovell, p. 75.
16. Jastrow, p. 53.
17. L. Barnett, *The Universe and Dr. Einstein* (New York: Harper and Brothers, 1948), p. 105.

CHAPTER 2

THE PROBABILITY OF A
SPONTANEOUS GENERATION OF LIFE

Introduction

In chapter 1 it was seen that the problem of origins is essentially philosophical in nature, and in that chapter we touched on the problem of cosmological origins. The remainder of the text will be devoted specifically to the problem of the origin of life on earth. Although this also reduces essentially to a metaphysical, theological, or philosophical problem, an attempt will be made here to deal with the problem in a forthright, practical manner.

Most people do not realize that the enigmatic and philosophical riddle of the ages is, in fact, the basis of our present gigantic space exploration effort. The philosophical basis of space exploration is elusive and almost escapes us because it is dwarfed by the sensationalism of the scientific and technological aspects of landing a man on the moon and the sending of unmanned space probes to the other planets of our solar system. At the end of the decade of the 1960s the United States had spent over twenty-four billion dollars in its national effort to get a man on the moon and was committed to the spending of many billions more. The accomplishment of the event resulted in an international political advantage for the United States, but underlying the sensationalism lay the riddle of the ages: How did life begin, and would a clue to the origin of life on earth be found in the moon rocks? No one who has followed closely our space efforts can question this emphasis on the problem of the origin of life on earth. Recently a group of space scientists urged immediate vigorous planning for a national effort to land unmanned spacecraft on the five outer planets beginning in the late 1970s. These scientists said: "Such probing in the outer reaches of the sun's bailiwick might, among other things, provide new tips on how life actually evolved, at least on earth."[1] It is, indeed,

1. *Arkansas Gazette* (Little Rock) 4 August 1969, p. A-16.

interesting that there is burning within culturally, scientifically, and technologically advanced modern man a curiosity concerning his own origin that causes him to reach out with efforts incomparable to any events of his total past history. It is as if he is asking in endless sequence: "From whence did I come? . . . From whence did I come? . . ." To this enigma of the ages the Christian has the answer: "In the beginning God created the heavens and the earth."

Although the problem of man's origin is basically philosophical, there have been numerous attempts by scientists to answer the question of the origin of life by experimental methods. In the final analysis, however, it is only possible by scientific investigation for one to be enabled to say, "Mechanistically life *could* have originated this way or it *could* have originated that way." *It is not within the province of science to rule out the theological creation alternative.* For the remainder of our series of study, we will be primarily concerned with what science has been able to contribute regarding the problem of the origin of life on earth. However, we will not be able to ignore entirely the philosophical overtones of the problem.

Definitions of "Life" and "Living"

There is no general agreement among the students of philosophy, biology, and biochemistry as to what constitutes a "living system." Some attribute the life principle to a simple inorganic reaction such as hydrogen combining with oxygen to give water. Others say that common table salt or even the sun is "alive," and others more sensibly attribute life only to those biological systems that move, respond to stimuli, reproduce, and carry on those other processes commonly associated with "life." Biologists generally limit themselves to an operational definition of life, stating descriptive characteristics such as growth, metabolism, reproduction, movement, organization, responsiveness, and adaptation.

There is no sharp line of demarcation between the living and the nonliving. This is seen as neither a triumph for mechanistic materialism nor for the creationist, though it does fit neatly into the origin-of-life scheme as visualized by the materialist. To us, plants, animals, and bacteria are alive; rocks, minerals, and simple **bio-organic** molecules are not alive. But what of the **viruses?** Do they represent marginal life—the transitional phase between the living and the nonliving? Viruses are not generally considered alive, but they are evidently marginal in respect to their being alive. Viruses may be crystallized, purified, and stored for apparently indefinite periods. However, they are totally incapable of performing the "normal" functions of living cells. They are parasiticlike particles and are propagated only by invading and taking over the reproductive machinery of normal cells and causing the latter to manufacture more virus particles. Virus particles evidently contain information coded within their molecules of **deoxyribonucleic acid (DNA)** or **ribonucleic acid (RNA)** which enables them, in a molecular sense, to communicate with the normal cell. The question reduces to this: Whether one regards the viruses as living or nonliving depends on one's particular definition of life.

When one finds a serious attempt to define life in physical terms he discovers that the definition is generally quite nebulous, as is the following by J. D. Bernal, professor of X-ray crystallography at the University of London, and one of the leading authorities in this area of thought: "My provisional definition of life: *Life is a partial, continuous, progressive, multiform and conditionally interactive, self-realization of the potentialities of atomic electron states.*"[2] (Italics, Bernal.) Bernal's definition of life is a materialistic definition. Life, according to him, is solely the result of the self-thrusting forces inherent within matter and matter alone. In terms of Figure 3, page 18, Bernal seems to say that there is nothing about life which originates outside the circle of materialism.

Bernal's definition is quite consistent with the less verbose, yet more pointed definition suggested by N. J. Berrill, professor of zoology at McGill University: "Life can be thought of as water kept at the right temperature in the right atmosphere in the right light for a long enough period of time."[3]

A. I. Oparin, a Russian biochemist who may well be regarded as the father of modern theories on the origin of life, gave life and its materialistic origin a dialectical interpretation:

---

2. J. D. Bernal, *The Origin of Life* (New York: Universe Books, Publisher, 1967), p. xv. Quote is repeated on p. 168.
3. N. J. Berrill, *You and the Universe* (New York: Dodd, Mead, & Co., Inc., 1958), p. 117.

A completely different prospect opens out before us if we try
to approach a solution of the problem dialectically rather than
metaphysically, on the basis of the successive changes in matter which preceded the appearance of life and led to its
emergence. . . . Life thus appears as a particular very complicated form of the motion of matter, arising as a new property
at a definite stage in the general development of matter.[4]

Oparin's resort to dialectical philosophy correctly points out that philosophical (if not theological) considerations underlie any approach to an
explanation of how life originated on earth. The philosophical aspects of
this problem are, however, generally inappropriately ignored. Oparin's
ideas first appeared in 1924 in a booklet entitled *The Origin of Life,* and
he has continued to make major contributions in this area of investigation
and thought. J. B. S. Haldane independently arrived at essentially the ideas
of Oparin and he suggested in 1929 that life arose on the primeval earth
from the interaction of organic chemicals in the earth's **pre-biotic** oceans.

Haldane's ideas, as well as those of Oparin, follow the philosophy of
dialectical materialism, which was originated by Karl Marx and Friedrich
Engels as an application of Hegel's logical method (dialectic) to philosophical materialism. The thought here, relative to the origin of life, is that
originally inorganic molecules were in collision (tension) with other inorganic molecules in such a way that the result was the synthesis of simple
bio-organic molecules. Subsequent collisions among the bio-organic molecules led to increasingly complex organic molecules and finally to the
inevitable synthesis of life. Life, therefore, according to the dialectical
material view, is a special manifestation of the motion of matter which
resulted from a natural series of stages in the development of matter.
Oparin argues that when life appeared, the old laws of physics and
chemistry continued to operate but they were supplemented by new
biological laws which previously did not exist.[5] The approach of dialectical materialism to the problem of the origin of life is thoroughly atheistic
in philosophy and may be visualized as proceeding according to the
oversimplified diagram shown in Figure 8. In the pages which follow, we

4. A. I. Oparin, *Origin of Life on the Earth* (New York: Academic Press, 1957), pp.
xi, xii.
5. A. I. Oparin, *Life—Its Nature, Origin, and Development* (New York: Academic
Press, Inc., 1962), p. 6.

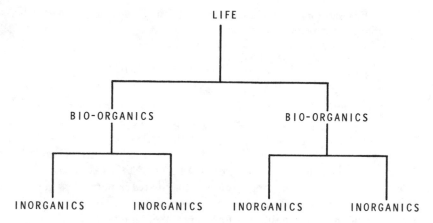

Fig. 8.   The dialectical materialistic scheme for the origin of life

will see that the philosophy of dialectical materialism has thoroughly permeated the thinking of modern scientists who propose mechanistic hypotheses for the origin of life on earth.

The position that is taken in this text is that life, in general, must be given an operational definition. We do not attempt to define life in terms of *what it is* but rather *what it does.* However, we maintain that life's origin is more than merely a special manifestation of the motion of matter; it was, in fact, a result of the divine command. God commanded and matter responded. We cannot say precisely how or by what mechanism matter responded. This we cannot know without revelation, and the nature of the problem precludes our ever knowing independently of divine revelation. Furthermore, we maintain that, as far as possible, the biochemistry and physiology of bacterial cells, a blade of grass, and the human mind must be approached by all scientists, including Christians, from a mechanistic point of view. However, the point of distinction is that the Christian approach is not from a mechanistic *material* point of view; it is from a mechanistic *theistic* point of view. The origin of life, as well as all natural law governing life, is attributed to the divine command. The Christian scientist does not hesitate to interpret such things as photosynthesis, respiration, the cause of cancer, strokes, and heart failure mechanistically. In the final analysis, he recognizes that he is merely describing the operation of the natural, biological laws created and upheld by God. Furthermore, he gives God praise for it all. Teleology is perfectly acceptable as an explanation of final causes.

Spontaneous Generation of Life

History shows that the problem of the origin of life has tantalized the mind of man for ages. The ancient Greeks proposed various explanations for the multiform presence of life on earth. Anaxagoras (510-428 B.C.) supposed that seeds of life (*spermata*) fell to earth with the rain and thus life sprang from these seeds. Aristotle (384-322 B.C.) believed that fleas, mosquitoes, worms, fishes, frogs, and mice originated in putrefying matter, filth, and moist soil. Even man was supposed to have had a similar wormlike origin. This is the classical concept of spontaneous generation which, during the Middle Ages, took on the distinction of an "established fact" of science; for opposing Aristotle was to defy the reasoning processes of the mind and to challenge established religious authority of the day. Theologians even claimed that Scripture verified this view inasmuch as in Genesis 1 it could be found that God said: "Let the earth bring forth—and the earth brought forth;—and God said, Let the waters bring forth—and the waters brought forth—living creatures."

Even today we are not completely divorced from this ancient concept of spontaneous generation. In some areas of the United States, it is still believed that placing a hair from a horse's tail in water will result in the hair turning into a snakelike worm.

Alchemists believed that a miniature man, called a homunculus, could be produced in a laboratory flask; and, with the invention of low-powered microscopes, some scientists affirmed that they could see the miniature man in human sperm. Drawings of these miniature "manikins" in human sperm were preserved as testimony to this concept of man's origin. Geese were supposed by some to grow on trees and lambs were thought to spring from gourdlike fruit. These deductions were particularly convenient for avowed vegetarians.

Francesco Redi (1626-1698) was the first to challenge the classical concept of spontaneous generation of life by use of experimental methods. He placed pieces of meat in a flask and covered it securely with gauze. White maggots developed from eggs deposited on the gauze by flies but no maggots developed from the meat itself. Leeuwenhoek (1632-1723), Buffon (1707-1799), and other noted scientists of this period made claims for and against classical spontaneous generation of life.

The controversy reached a peak about 1860 and the French Academy of Sciences offered a prize to the person who would settle the issue of spontaneous generation. Louis Pasteur (1822-1895) accepted the challenge and in 1864 was awarded the prize. He had effectively demonstrated once and for all that life does not spontaneously arise from putrefying matter, filth, moist soil, and such substances. At the same time, Pasteur succeeded in laying the basic foundation for the "germ theory" of disease. During succeeding years he introduced the concept of "pasteurizing" milk and other foods by making them germ free by heating to kill the germs. Pasteur's experiments sounded the death knell for classical spontaneous generation of life; but, as we shall soon see, the materialist has revived a new concept of spontaneous generation.

The New Concept of Spontaneous Generation

The new concept of spontaneous generation is even more incredible than that which was disproved by Pasteur. Instead of supposing that life originated in murky waters, putrefying flesh, and moist soil, the materialist supposes that in the distant past—presumably some 3.5 billion years ago—inorganic molecules reacted with inorganic molecules to produce a variety of bio-organic molecules which were the molecular precursors of life. It is then supposed that over long periods of time the chance combination of these bio-organic molecules, either in dilute, primeval oceans or else on mud clays, resulted in the formation of primordial life. Hence the spontaneous generation of life.

Before we examine the probability or improbability of spontaneous generation, let us again remember the framework within which the materialist reasons. His thought in these matters follows this sequence:

Presupposition:	Matter is the only eternal principle.
Observation:	Here we are.
Conclusion:	Spontaneous generation of life occurred.

Now, let us consider the likelihood that life could have arisen spontaneously as visualized by the materialists.

A Qualitative Treatment of the
Probability of the Spontaneous Generation of Life

Before we can attempt a semiquantitative treatment of the probability of spontaneous generation, we must first view the problem qualitatively as well as improve our overall insights into the nature of the problem. All of the following speculations as to the probability of spontaneous generation are taken from leading authorities in this area of thought. All authors quoted are advocates of a mechanistic material approach to the problem. Some virtually admit its impossibility, others express grave skepticism as to its likelihood, and one is so positive in his thinking that he advocates that the spontaneous generation of life be enunciated as the fourth law of thermodynamics.

The scientific use of the word *spontaneous* should be clearly understood. Spontaneity has no reference whatsoever to the time required for an event to take place. Long periods of time are required for some spontaneous processes to occur, whereas other spontaneous processes occur rapidly. A spontaneous reaction or process is one that occurs freely and without constraint; it is a process that does not require any external force in order for the event to occur, irrespective of the time involved. For example, a ball rolls down an inclined plane freely and without assistance from any force other than the natural force of gravity. Whether the ball rolls rapidly or slowly is immaterial; the fact that it rolls freely means that the event is spontaneous.

Hence, the term "spontaneous generation of life" means that life came into being by matter being motivated not by any force external to the material world but only by those forces which are inherent within matter itself. The term means that matter moved, matter organized, and matter became living, with the process occurring freely and without assistance from any force independent of matter. An adherent to a theory of spontaneous generation of life must necessarily either completely ignore the role of the supernatural in the origin of life or else deny the existence of the supernatural; for, if a force independent of matter is involved, then the process can no longer be spontaneous.

The question arises as to whether the supernatural could have functioned in merely ordering matter in such a way that it was conducive for appropriate processes to occur which would have led to the emergence of life. The answer is yes, if one wants to think of God as somewhat of a superbiochemist. However, such a concept would not be consistent with the scientific use of the word *spontaneous*. Use of that word in reference to the generation of life precludes an ordering force independent of matter itself. Creation and spontaneous generation are mutually exclusive.

As has already been pointed out, Pasteur's experiments showed that spontaneous generation of life does not occur, at least in the classical sense. But the materialists have now returned to the once discarded hypothesis with the modification that Pasteur, of course, did not prove that spontaneous generation of life did not occur *at one time*. Haynes and Hanawalt, commenting on an article on the origin of life by Harvard University professor and Nobel Prize winner, George Wald, make the following comment:

> The present generally accepted view of the origin of life is none other than the old theory of "spontaneous generation" in a modern guise. But, as Wald notes, today's version attributes the beginning of life to perfectly natural phenomena.[6]

In Wald's article he verified the claim made earlier that the materialists have now returned to a concept of spontaneous generation of life:

> I think a scientist has no choice but to approach the origin of life through a hypothesis of spontaneous generation.[7]

Wald's following statement is particularly interesting:

> One has only to contemplate the magnitude of this task (evolution of primeval life from inorganics) to concede that the spontaneous generation of a living organism is impossible. Yet here we are—as a result, I believe, of spontaneous generation.[8]

This admission that spontaneous generation of life is impossible, yet we are here on earth as the result of spontaneous generation, is most relevant to our present discussion. It might be added that such faith we have not seen, no, not in all of materialism. Wald is, of course, reasoning within the materialistic framework of thought. His reasoning seems to follow the sequence suggested earlier:

6. R. H. Haynes and P. C. Hanawalt, eds., *The Molecular Basis of Life* (San Francisco: W. H. Freeman and Co., n.d.), p. 293.
7. Haynes and Hanawalt, p. 339.
8. Haynes and Hanawalt.

Presupposition: Matter is the only eternal principle.
Observation: Here we are.
Conclusion: Spontaneous generation of life occurred.

Wald goes on in his article to interpret "impossible" to mean so mathematically improbable as to cause one to say that it is "practically" impossible. He argues that so long as the probability is not zero then the event must occur, given indefinite time. He states:

> In this colloquial, practical sense I concede the spontaneous origin of life to be "impossible." It is impossible as we judge events in the scale of human experience.[9]

But is it true that, given indefinite time, any event of low probability is inevitable? This is a most critical question and we will attempt to answer it shortly.

John Keosian, Rutgers University biology professor, acknowledges the difficulty in conceiving that a living thing could arise by chance:

> Even conceptually it is difficult to see how a system satisfying the minimum criteria for a living thing can arise by chance and, simultaneously, include a mechanism containing the suitable information for its own replication.[10]

Others, however, such as physiologists Loewy and Siekevitz, claim that the spontaneous generation of life is so certain it should be enunciated as the fourth law of thermodynamics:

> We should perhaps enunciate a "fourth law," (of thermodynamics) which would state that, given plenty of time, the necessary atomic building blocks, the right temperature, and a steady supply of free energy possibly fluctuating in a diurnal cycle, a "bios" of increasing complexity will of necessity develop, which has the over-all effect of decreasing the rate at which free energy becomes degraded. . . . We no longer think of evolution as the "great coincidence," but as a full-fledged law of nature.[11]

9. Haynes and Hanawalt, p. 340.
10. From *The Origin of Life* by John Keosian © 1964 and 1968 by Litton Educational Publishing, Inc. Reprinted by permission of Van Nostrand Reinhold Company.
11. A. G. Loewy and P. Siekevitz, *Cell Structure and Function* (New York: Holt, Rinehart, and Winston, Inc., 1963), p. 9.

J. D. Bernal, doubtless one of the leading voices in this area of thought, acknowledges that the study of the origin of life raises more questions than it answers. He further acknowledges, "The question of the origin of life is essentially speculative." Particular attention should be given to the following statement by Bernal. He is commenting on ultraskepticism and the improbability of the spontaneous generation of life:

> The latter of these is the more difficult to refute. By applying the strict canons of scientific method to this subject, it is possible to demonstrate effectively at several places in the story, how life could not have arisen; the improbabilities are too great, the chances of the emergence of life too small. Regrettably from this point of view, life is here on Earth in all its multiplicity of forms and activities and the arguments have to be bent around to support its existence.[12]

It is interesting that Bernal, who looks at the origin-of-life problem purely from a materialistic point of view, says that it is regrettable that life exists on earth because the probability of its spontaneously arising is so small. He seems to be saying, "Since one cannot satisfactorily explain life materialistically, it is regrettable that life exists!" This is, of course, a natural consequence of the denial of the theistic alternative. Bernal goes on to summarize the present unsolved problems associated with a materialistic explanation of the origin of life in the following seven categories:[13]

1. The occurrence of sustained metabolism;
2. The origin of chirality (right- and left-handedness of many bio-organic molecules);
3. The occurrence of **homo-** and **hetero-polymerization**;
4. The replication of order in hetero-polymers;
5. The primacy of indefinitely extended life over the earlier formation of organisms;
6. The first genesis of membranes;
7. The heterogeneous origin of the cell from different organelles and the evolution of their mutual control.

One does not have to be very observant to recognize that if the above seven areas of the origin-of-life problem remain unsolved, then this is tantamount to saying that virtually no significant progress has been made by the materialist in regard to this problem. Nevertheless, some progress

12. Bernal, pp. xvi, 2, 120.
13. Bernal, p. 156.

has been made by the materialist and the extent of this progress will be reviewed in chapters 3 and 4.

Chemists Green and Goldberger emphatically claim that present available facts do not provide even so much as a basis for postulating that living cells arose on the planet Earth:

> How, then, did the precursor cell arise? The only unequivocal rejoinder to this question is that we do not know. Undoubtedly, selection played a role in the process, although the efficiency was probably not as great as in Darwinian evolution.
>
> However, the macromolecule-to-cell transition is a jump of fantastic dimensions, which lies beyond the range of testable hypothesis. In this area all is conjecture. The available facts do not provide a basis for postulating that cells arose on this planet.[14]

In concluding his book *The Implications of Evolution,* physiologist and biochemist G. A. Kerkut has the following statement to make regarding the spontaneous generation of life:

> It is therefore a matter of faith on the part of the biologist that biogenesis* did occur and he can choose whatever method of biogenesis happens to suit him personally; the evidence for what did happen is not available.[15]

It is now appropriate to ask if a scientist has another choice but to approach the problem of the origin of life through a hypothesis of spontaneous generation. It is our conclusion that the scientist who is also a Christian has no choice but to rule out spontaneity as an essential element in the creation event. "Spontaneity" and "creation" are mutually exclusive terms. If a creator had any role whatsoever to play in the origin of life on earth, then the event was not a spontaneous event by the very definition of the term spontaneous.

---

*Kerkut's use of the word *biogenesis* here is not clearly understood. The word technically means "life coming from preexisting life"; however, the above statement was made in the context of a discussion on spontaneous generation.

14. D. E. Green and R. F. Goldberger, *Molecular Insights into the Living Process* (New York: Academic Press, 1967), pp. 403, 407.
15. G. A. Kerkut, *Implications of Evolution* (Oxford: Pergamon Press, 1960), p. 150.

A completely quantitative treatment of the probability of spontaneous generation is impossible. Even a semiquantitative analysis of the problem would be unwise until after we have studied the complexity of the simplest living things as well as those steps invoked by mechanistic materialism to explain the development of primordial life. Hence, we will postpone a discussion of a semiquantitative treatment of spontaneous generation until chapter 4.

If life did not spontaneously arise on earth, and if it was not created by divine intervention, then only one logical alternative remains. That is that life has eternally existed. This is the idea known as "panspermia" and will be considered next.

Life on Other Worlds?

In the preceding discussion on cosmological origins it was pointed out that the oscillating universe and steady-state hypotheses were advanced, in part, to avoid the necessity of a beginning or time zero. The hypotheses simply maintain that matter has existed eternally. Panspermia is an origin-of-life hypothesis that has taken on several forms, but the essence of each is that the living biological system is as eternal as matter itself. Here, also, is the chief weakness of this theory; it simply begs the question of biological origins and avoids the issue.

One aspect of the concept of panspermia holds that germs of life dropped to the earth—a suitable host for life—from interplanetary space in the form of viable spores or microorganisms. Another approach is that viable spores of life were brought to the earth from outer space by meteorites. Recent impetus has been given the hypothesis of panspermia by the discovery of radiation from space that is attributed to simple organic molecules.[16] These investigators have apparently discovered formaldehyde, ammonia, and water in intergalactic space by use of the 140-foot parabolic antenna radiotelescope at Green Bank, West Virginia. This has created renewed interest in the theory that life originated on earth by a viable life spore falling to earth from an intergalactic "biocloud." Commenting on the motivation for probing intergalactic space for organic molecules, these investigators state: "The motivating force behind the search bears on theories on the origin of life."[17] Many authors

16. *Chemical and Engineering News,* 31 March 1969, p. 11.
17. *Chemical and Engineering News.*

have recognized the great improbability that a viable spore could have survived interplanetary radiation. Haynes and Hanawalt, for example, state the following commonly held opinion:

> Furthermore, it is now realized that it would have been virtually impossible even for a bacterial spore to survive the radiation received during a long trip through space.[18]

As suggested earlier, it is rather common knowledge that the primary purpose behind the present moon and planetary explorations is a quest for an answer to the problem of the origin of life. As Charlie Brown would say, "The philosophical implications of this alone are staggering." Over one hundred laboratories the world over have already analyzed the lunar rocks returned by Apollo 11 and Apollo 12 moon missions. A primary concern in these analytical procedures is a search for residues of living biological systems. It has long been a controversial matter as to whether carbon compounds *of biological origin* have been found in meteorites.[19] Certainly one of the world's most authoritative voices on the question of biomolecules in meteorites and lunar samples is NASA's Dr. Cyril Ponnamperuma. As recently as December 1970 he stated: "But to date, available evidence as to the indigenous presence of such biomolecules in meteorites or in the lunar samples is inconclusive."[20] About six months after the above statement was released, Ponnamperuma and other NASA scientists at Ames Research Center announced the discovery of some six amino acids common to the normal living cell in two different meteorites. One of the meteorites fell at Murray, Kentucky, in 1950 and the other fell at Murchison, Victoria, Australia, in 1969. Both are believed to be about 4.5 billion years old. NASA reported that this discovery "appears to be the first conclusive proof of extra terrestrial chemical evolution."[21] None of these organic substances is thought to be biological in origin. It also should be pointed out that the quantities of organic compounds discovered in the meteorites are ultraminute.

It should be noted that, if the theory of panspermia has any validity, then one would expect the moon's surface to contain at least residues from "viable life spores" from the hypothetical intergalactic "biocloud,"

18. Haynes and Hanawalt, p. 292.
19. B. Mason, "Organic Matter from Space," *Scientific American*, March 1963, p. 43.
20. *Chemical and Engineering News*, 7 December 1970, p. 16.
21. *Arkansas Gazette* (Little Rock) 19 June 1971, p. A-7.

as well as spores of life which possibly escaped earth's gravity and were deposited on the moon as the moon passed through the earth's orbit around the sun. These expectations accounted for the quarantine precautions which were taken on the return of the astronauts from the moon's surface. The failure thus far to find traces of viable life spores or bio-organics on the moon has been a severe blow to the theory of panspermia.

Table 1[22] summarizes the results obtained in numerous chemical searches for organic material in moon samples obtained by the Apollo 11 mission. In short, it is safe to conclude that analyses on lunar samples obtained by the Apollo 11 mission allow absolutely no justification for saying that either life or the simplest of bio-organic molecules are indigenous to the lunar surface. Any bio-organics found in the analyses are in such small quantities that they can safely be attributed to either the handling of the samples or else to the burning of lunar module rocket fuel. We have, therefore, to this date, absolutely no evidence—large or small—that life exists or has ever existed anywhere in the universe except on the planet Earth.

Nevertheless, speculations continue as to the existence of life on other planets within our solar system and elsewhere in the universe. Within our planetary system, Mars and Venus are the only two planets besides Earth which have seriously been considered as candidates for supporting life. Recent space probes have disclosed that Mars is a cold, barren, almost atmosphereless planet whose surface would surely be hostile to life. Regarding the possibility of life on Mars, Dr. Norman H. Horowitz, professor of biology at Caltech, states: "If life does exist on Mars, it must be something very primitive, like Bacteria; the idea of substantial plants or animals is out."[23] As for Venus, it is an inferno where surface temperatures at the equator reach 1,000° F., a temperature so hot that it would melt lead, tin, and zinc metals. Life there, even of a very primitive sort, is unimaginable except by the most desperate materialists. So far, each successive planetary space probe has pushed us closer to the conclusion that life on the planet Earth is a unique occurrence within the planetary system of our sun.

22. *Science*, 30 January 1970.
23. Kenneth F. Weaver, "Voyage to the Planets," *National Geographic*, Vol. 138, No. 2 (August 1970), p. 169.

MATERIALS SEARCHED FOR	RESULTS OBTAINED
Carbon	200 parts per million as carbon monoxide.
Alkanes, C_{15} -C_{30}	None above one part per billion.
Organic compounds	None indigenous to lunar surface.
Organic compounds	Some low molecular weight alkanes, no bio-organics.
Organic compounds	None above one part per million.
Methane	One part per million only.
Total organic carbon	Less than 10 parts per million.
Carbon, nitrogen, phosphorus, and sulfur	Five to 4,200 parts per million.
Bio-organic compounds	None but that were not possibly formed by burning rocket fuel.
Porphyrins	None at a level of 10^{-13} mole/gram.
Porphyrins	10^{-10} grams/gram of lunar dust found but attributed to burning rocket fuel.
Microfossils	Conclusion: Lunar surface has always been devoid of life.
Microfossils	No evidence of indigenous biological activity.
Viable organisms	None, only colored inorganic artifacts; sample was tested in 300 separate environments.

Table 1.   Summary of results obtained from the analysis of Apollo 11 moon rocks

As for the possibility of life on other planetary systems, the fact is that we do not even know for certain that there are other planets associated with other stars in the universe. At best we have only indirect evidence that one or two stars other than our sun have a planet encircling them. Whether or not planetary systems are ordinary or extraordinary occurrences depends on the manner in which galaxies, stars, and planets came into being. If they were divinely created, then it is totally a matter of the prerogative of God as to the number of planetary systems He chose to create. Furthermore, He could have created life on as many planets as He desired and could have made possible redemption and salvation for other intelligent planetary inhabitants. Mechanistically, we do not know; and we stand very little chance of ever knowing for sure how the galaxies, stars, and our solar system came into existence. In the meantime, any speculation as to imaginary men on imaginary planets is purely idle speculation.

As pointed out earlier, our sun's nearest star neighbor is Alpha Centauri, which is four and one-half light years away. At this distance an observer on a planet of Alpha Centauri would see our sun as a fairly bright star; but even Jupiter, the largest of our planets, would be lost in the glare of the brilliance of the sun and could not be seen. According to M. I. T. astronomer O. Struve, Jupiter could only be seen by "long photographic exposures with the largest existing telescopes if the glare of the sun could somehow be eliminated, which, of course, cannot now be accomplished."[24] Of the some 200 billion stars in our galaxy there are only a few within twenty light years of our solar system.

At present it is highly unlikely that we can know for certain in the foreseeable future whether any of these stars have planetary systems capable of sustaining life. The probability that any one of these imaginary planets sponsors life has become vanishingly small.[25] Furthermore, the probability that we will ever discover for certain whether or not life exists elsewhere in the universe is so small that for practical purposes it may be regarded as zero. However, if life was discovered elsewhere, this should not disturb the faith of the Christian. One certainly does not want to limit God's creative acts to the planet Earth, and we know of no Scripture which directly or by inference would exclude God having created life elsewhere in the universe. However, the Christian can spend his time much

---

24. O. Struve, *The Universe* (Cambridge, Mass.: The M. I. T. Press, 1962), p. 9.
25. Struve, p. 159.

more profitably by focusing his energies on the tasks he has to perform on earth rather than idly speculating about imaginary men on imaginary planets. He should, however, guard against so orienting his thoughts in this area that it would cause his faith in God to be shaken should life be discovered elsewhere in the universe.

CHAPTER 3

THE COMPLEXITY OF THE
SIMPLEST LIVING THINGS

Introduction

The advocates of the new concept of the spontaneous generation of life propose that the first living thing resulted from a gradual evolution of matter from simple atoms and molecules to a complex organization of matter which became "alive." These changes are supposed to have occurred independent of any force outside the material realm. Figure 9

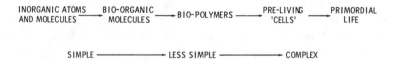

Fig. 9.   The materialistic origin-of-life hypothesis

illustrates the origin-of-life scheme normally advocated by mechanistic materialists. In the gradual development of matter from the simple to the complex, it is apparent that the first or primordial living cells would have represented life at its simplest possible state of organization. In other words, it would have been life in an *ultimately or absolutely simple state.* Yet, in order to be alive this mass of matter would have necessarily exhibited the characteristics of life listed in chapter 2. These characteristics are *growth, metabolism, reproduction, movement, organization, responsiveness,* and *adaptation.* It is inconceivable that even the simplest form of life could have by-passed any one of these characteristics. Had the evolving primordial cell been too simple to exhibit any one of these characteristics, it could not have been alive. Indeed, the original living cell would have been simple, relative to bacteria or algae, but by necessity it must have been *ultimately simple.* Only by some sort of creative miracle, which the materialists are unwilling to accept, could a *relatively simple* cell

51

such as a bacterium or algae have spontaneously arisen as the original or primordial cell. In this chapter we will attempt to specify the degree of complexity which would be possessed by an ultimately or absolutely simple living thing.

The following statement was made by Johns Hopkins biochemist and cellular energetics expert A. L. Lehninger:

> A living cell is inherently an unstable and improbable organization; it maintains the beautifully complex and specific orderliness of its fragile structure only by the constant use of energy.[1]

This is a true statement and, according to current thought, it must apply to all living cells—past, present, and future. It must, therefore, partially describe the original or primordial cell as postulated by mechanistic materialism. Admittedly then, the first living cell would have been inherently an unstable and improbable organization. But can we specify the minimal complexity possessed by this improbable organization? Current biophysicists think the answer to this question is yes. However, as we will now see, the absolute simplicity of the hypothetical primordial cell represents a degree of complexity that is staggering to the imagination. It is our thesis here that it is preposterous to suppose that such an improbable organization arose spontaneously, even if it arose at all.

Viruses

As stated earlier, viruses do not exhibit all of the above characteristics of living things and are not normally regarded as living. Viruses notably do not exhibit growth and reproduction independent of other living cells. Though we may safely dismiss viruses as living, we must reckon with the fact that they are marginal in respect to their being alive. From one viewpoint of mechanistic materialism, viruses were possibly a "stepping stone" on which matter touched on its evolution to become a viable, primordial thing capable of exhibiting all of life's properties. Viruses, like simple organic molecules and even inorganic minerals, take on several

---

1. A. L. Lehninger, "How Cells Transform Energy," *Scientific American*, Vol. 205, No. 3 (September 1961), p. 63.

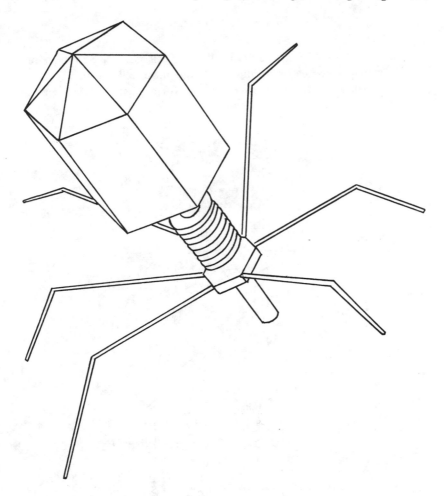

Fig. 10. A drawing of the T2 bacteriophage

different geometrical shapes. A drawing of a rather complex virus particle based on an electron photomicrograph is shown in Figure 10. Other viruses are cylindrical, spherical, spiral, or otherwise possess any of a variety of complex geometrical, polygonal shapes. Some viruses are composed of concentric spheres, and others (for example, the influenza virus) possess a spiral structure within a sphere. Chemically speaking, viruses are composed principally of **protein** and **DNA** or **RNA**.

A "Typical" Cell

There is no such thing as a "typical" living cell. Cells vary considerably in their shapes and constitutions. However, most cells possess the sub-cellular composition shown diagrammatically in Figure 11.* Even the

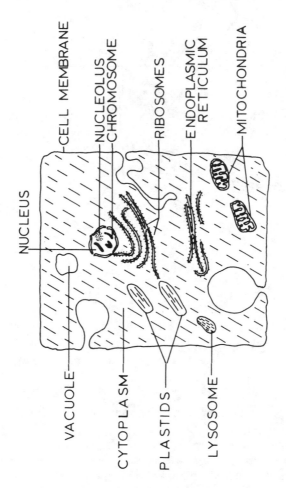

Fig. 11.   A drawing of a "typical" living cell

A brief statement of the nature and function of each sub-cellular organelle is given in the glossary.

simplest of living cells is awesome in complexity. Most certainly the primordial living cell, as considered by the materialists, would have possessed a complexity somewhere between that of a virus and the typical living cell shown above.

The PPLO

Since the primordial cell as recognized by the materialists was likely something between a virus as shown in Figure 10 and a typical cell as shown in Figure 11, then it is proper for us to look for a free-living cell intermediate between the virus and the typical cell. By "free-living" is meant the ability of the cell to feed on a nonliving medium so as to reproduce to give two or more daughter cells which are replicas of itself.

The smallest known, and presumably the simplest, free-living cell is the pleuropneumonialike organism (PPLO).[2] The PPLO weighs approxi-

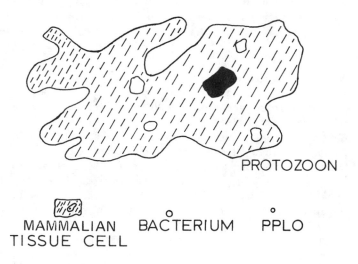

PROTOZOON

MAMMALIAN BACTERIUM PPLO
TISSUE CELL

Fig. 12. A comparison of the relative sizes of a protozoon, a mammalian tissue cell, a bacterium, and a PPLO

2. H. Morowitz and M. Tourtellotte, "The Smallest Living Cells," *Scientific American*, Vol. 206, No. 3 (March 1962), p. 117.

mately 5 x 10^{-16} grams, which is about a billion times less than a protozoon. It is approximately one-tenth the size of a bacterium. These figures mean very little to one who is not trained to think in the terms given. However, we can all appreciate diagrams of relative sizes. In Figure 12, the relative sizes of a protozoon, a mammalian tissue cell, a bacterium, and a PPLO are given.[3] On the same scale we would not be able to even see a large molecule and certainly not an atom. For this reason, in Figure 13 we have enlarged the PPLO size to show the relative sizes of the PPLO elementary body, the theoretically smallest hypothetical cell, a large molecule, a small molecule (monomer unit), and an atom.[4]

The elementary body is essentially a PPLO daughter cell. The size of the hypothetical cell is theoretically the absolute lower limit which a cell could possess due to mathematical restrictions imposed by essential life properties. For example, a cell must possess a cell membrane, a cell must be equipped with a minimum number of enzymatically catalyzed reactions, and there must be a reasonable volume of space enclosing the molecular constituents of the cell. Theoretical physicists and biologists agree that the smallest conceivable cell would be perhaps 500 angstroms in diameter.[5] Of a cell this size, biophysicists Morowitz and Tourtellotte assert:

> A cell of this size would have, in its nonaqueous substance, about 1.5 million atoms. Combined in groups of about 20 each, these atoms would form 75,000 amino acids and nucleotides, the building blocks from which the large molecules of the cell's metabolic and reproductive apparatus would be composed. Since these large molecules each incorporate about 500 building blocks, the cell would have a complement of 150 large molecules. This purely theoretical cell would be delicate in the extreme, its ability to reproduce successfully always threatened by the random thermal motion of its constituents.[6]

This hypothetical cell would represent the *absolute simplicity* of the smallest and simplest living thing. Yet, it is utterly complex. It is inconceivable, except to the most persistent materialist, that probability and

---

3. Morowitz and Tourtellotte, p. 119.
4. Morowitz and Tourtellotte, p. 123.
5. Morowitz and Tourtellotte, p. 124.
6. Morowitz and Tourtellotte, pp. 124, 126.

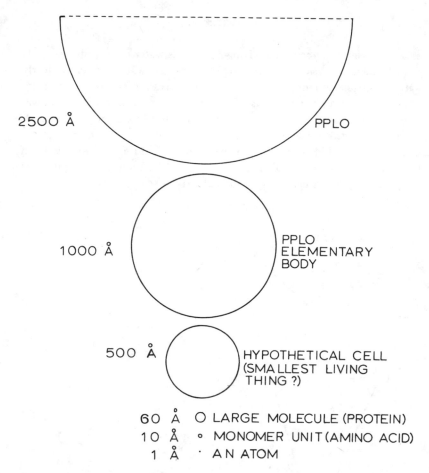

2500 Å   PPLO

1000 Å   PPLO
ELEMENTARY
BODY

500 Å   HYPOTHETICAL CELL
(SMALLEST LIVING
THING ?)

60 Å   O LARGE MOLECULE (PROTEIN)
10 Å   ∘ MONOMER UNIT (AMINO ACID)
1 Å   · AN ATOM

Fig. 13   A comparison of the relative sizes of a PPLO, PPLO
elementary body, the smallest hypothetical cell, a
large molecule, a monomer unit, and an atom

chance factors alone could slowly and spontaneously bring together the
component molecules necessary to construct such a cell.

Before we can fully appreciate the complexity of even the simplest
living cell, it is essential that we look at the molecules of which living cells
are composed. A hypothetical journey into a living cell would be as
staggering to our imagination as would a hypothetical journey into the
billions of galaxies of the starry heavens.

Water

About eighty percent of all living material is water. If there is a tangible miracle in the physical universe then it must be water. Water is clearly nature's singularly most unique substance, possessing at least twelve properties peculiar to itself in terms of magnitude and variation. This fact was first pointed out in a classic text published in 1913 by mechanist L. J. Henderson entitled *The Fitness of the Environment.*[7] Henderson's observations are as valid today as they were in 1913. Life, as we know it on earth, would not be possible if it were not for this unique combination of properties within a single simple molecule, H_2O.

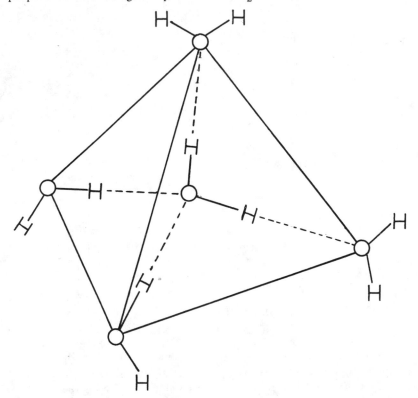

Fig. 14.   The water molecule showing intermolecular associations via hydrogen bonding

7. L. J. Henderson, *The Fitness of the Environment* (New York: Macmillan, 1913; republished, 1959 by P. Smith, Gloucester, Mass.)

For example, were we to predict the properties of water, basing our predictions on the properties of its nearest structural relatives, we would predict that water would be a gas at arctic and antarctic polar temperatures; it would possess an extremely disagreeable odor; and it would be one of nature's most poisonous substances. Of course, under these conditions, life would be impossible. Mysterious? Not necessarily. We can satisfactorily account for, in mechanistic terms, the unique properties of water by considering such factors as the distribution of electrons in the molecule, the shape of the molecule and, in particular, the oxygen-hydrogen bond lengths. But *why* precisely this shape and size for the combination of the two atoms of hydrogen and one oxygen and *why* precisely this distribution of electrons among the two hydrogens and one oxygen? Now this is a pretty big question because it is not within the province of science to answer *why* questions. To attempt to answer these questions is to transcend human intellect and to immediately find ourselves involved with philosophy, metaphysics, or theology. At this level of thought one may safely invoke teleology (purpose, design) for a final explanation. Water has precisely the shape, size, and electron distribution it does because it was designed this way. In other words, from the Christian point of view, this is the way God planned and designed the structure of the water molecule.

Slightly more complicated but immensely less interesting molecules are methane, CH_4; ammonia, NH_3; and carbon dioxide, CO_2. It is from these

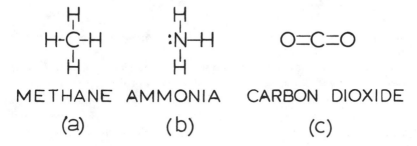

METHANE AMMONIA CARBON DIOXIDE

(a) (b) (c)

Fig. 15. (a) methane, (b) ammonia, and (c) carbon dioxide

simple molecules plus water and hydrogen gas that the materialist presumes that primordial life and all of its subsequent variant forms have arisen through slow, spontaneous evolutionary processes alone.

Bio-organic molecules, or molecules from which living systems are constructed, are infinitely more complex than the simple structures shown above. The **proteins, ribonucleic acids (DNA** and **RNA),** and **poly-**

saccharides are complex **polymers** of individual **monomer** units known as **amino acids, nucleotides,** and **monosaccharides** (sugars) respectively. The polymers (*poly,* "many"; *mer,* "part") are biological molecules of nearly incomprehensible size and complexity which are built up from unique combinations of monomer (*mono,* "one"; *mer,* "part") units. Hundreds of these giant molecules must be obtained before we can even begin to think in terms of a "living thing." We will now examine the means by which the amino acids are combined to give proteins, and the means by which nucleotides are combined to give the ribonucleic acids DNA and RNA.

Amino Acids to Proteins

In Figure 16 are shown the structures of three typical amino acids: glycine, alanine, and serine. In the structures for the latter two molecules the starred carbon atom represents a peculiar phenomenon of nature, asymmetry. This property causes some molecules to be "right-handed" while others are "left-handed." Such molecules bear a relationship to each other identical to the relationship that one's left hand has to one's right hand.

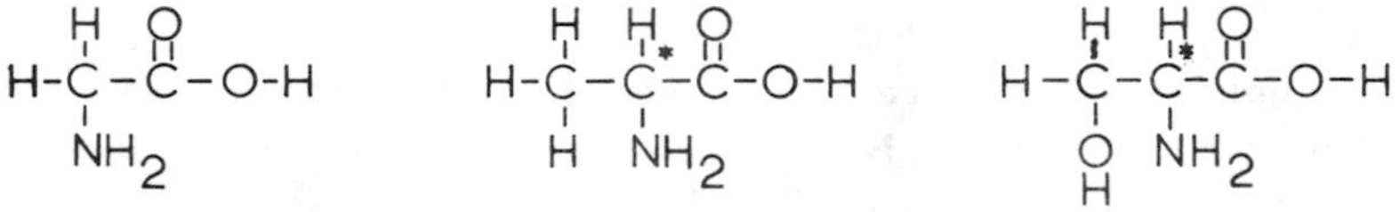

Fig. 16.   Amino acids: (a) glycine, (b) alanine, and (c) serine

Of the twenty fundamental amino acids (see glossary), only glycine does not possess this property of handedness. For some reason, still not clear to us, it is found almost exclusively that only left-handed molecules are used in the making of proteins from amino acids. Furthermore, it should be pointed out that a right-handed molecule cannot substitute for a left-handed molecule or vice versa in nature.

Peptides are made when a molecule of water is removed from amino acids and the latter are bonded by the way of "peptide" bonds (see Fig. 17). Proteins are polypeptides generally containing hundreds of individual amino acid molecules.

To further illustrate the complexity, but nevertheless the order, found in proteins, let us examine for a moment the hemoglobin molecule which functions in blood as a carrier of molecular oxygen. Now one person's

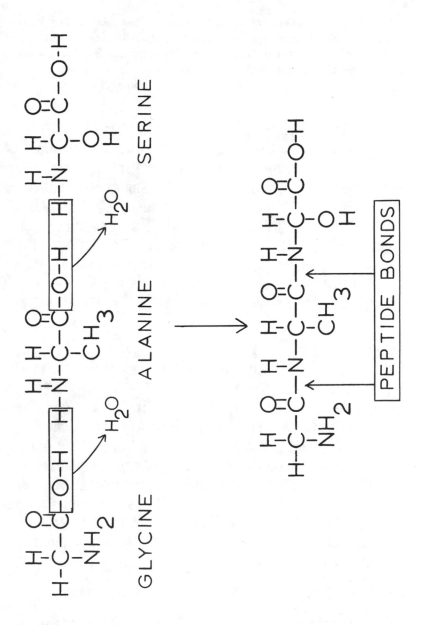

Fig. 17.   Formation of a tripeptide, glycylalanylserine

hemoglobin is the same as another person's hemoglobin; but human hemoglobin differs from that of apes, whales, and other animals, although all hemoglobin analyzed so far possesses certain similarities. Human hemoglobin consists of four molecules, two of an alpha type and two of a beta type, as shown in Figure 18. There are 141 amino acid molecules in the

Alpha chain
Val·Leu·Ser·Pro·Ala·Asp·Lys·Thr·Asn·Val·Lys·Ala·Ala·Try·
Gly·Lys·Val·Gly·Ala·His·Ala·Gly·Glu·Tyr·Gly·Ala·Glu·Ala·
Leu·Glu·Arg·Met·Phe·Leu·Ser·Phe·Pro·Thr·Thr·Lys·Thr·Tyr·
Phe·Pro·His·Phe·Asp·Leu·Ser·His·Gly·Ser·Ala·Gln·Val·Lys·
Gly·His·Gly·Lys·Lys·Val·Ala·Asp·Ala·Leu·Thr·Asn·Ala·Val·
Ala·His·Val·Asp·Asp·Met·Pro·Asn·Ala·Leu·Ser·Ala·Leu·Ser·
Asp·Leu·His·Ala·His·Lys·Leu·Arg·Val·Asp·Pro·Val·Asp·Phe·
Lys·Leu·Leu·Ser·His·Cys·Leu·Leu·Val·Thr·Leu·Ala·Ala·His·
Leu·Pro·Ala·Glu·Phe·Thr·Pro·Ala·Val·His·Ala·Ser·Leu·Asp·
Lys·Phe·Leu·Ala·Ser·Val·Ser·Thr·Val·Leu·Thr·Ser·Lys·Tyr·
Arg

Beta chain ↓
Val·His·Leu·Thr·Pro·Glu·Glu·Lys·Ser·Ala·Val·Thr·Ala·Leu·
Try·Gly·Lys·Val·Asn·Val·Asp·Glu·Val·Gly·Gly·Glu·Ala·Leu·
Gly·Arg·Leu·Leu·Val·Val·Tyr·Pro·Try·Thr·Gln·Arg·Phe·Phe·
Glu·Ser·Phe·Gly·Asp·Leu·Ser·Thr·Pro·Asp·Ala·Val·Met·Gly·
Asn·Pro·Lys·Val·Lys·Ala·His·Gly·Lys·Lys·Val·Leu·Gly·Ala·
Phe·Ser·Asp·Gly·Leu·Ala·His·Leu·Asp·Asn·Leu·Lys·Gly·Thr·
Phe·Ala·Thr·Leu·Ser·Glu·Leu·His·Cys·Asp·Lys·Leu·His·Val·
Asp·Pro·Glu·Asn·Phe·Arg·Leu·Leu·Gly·Asn·Val·Leu·Val·Cys·
Val·Leu·Ala·His·His·Phe·Gly·Lys·Gln·Phe·Thr·Pro·Pro·Val·
Gln·Ala·Ala·Tyr·Gln·Lys·Val·Val·Ala·Gly·Val·Ala·Asp·Ala·
Leu·Ala·His·Lys·Tyr·His

Fig. 18.   Alpha and beta chains of human hemoglobin

alpha chain and 146 amino acid molecules in the beta chain. Sickle cell anemia is an inherited disease in which the only difference between normal and pathological hemoglobin is the substitution of a valine amino acid for a glutamic acid amino acid in the sixth position from the N-terminus of the beta peptide chain (see arrow in Fig. 18). This is the substitution of two amino acids (one from each beta chain) in a total of 574 amino acids in the hemoglobin molecule! However, this is still not the total structure of hemoglobin. The functional part of the molecule, in respect to the carrying of oxygen, is an iron atom found in a nonprotein fragment known as the heme group. There are four of these per molecule of human hemoglobin. The structure of the heme group is shown in Figure 19. This structure is the basic pattern of a class of bio-organic molecules known as **porphyrins**. Though it is only the iron atom that "functions" in the

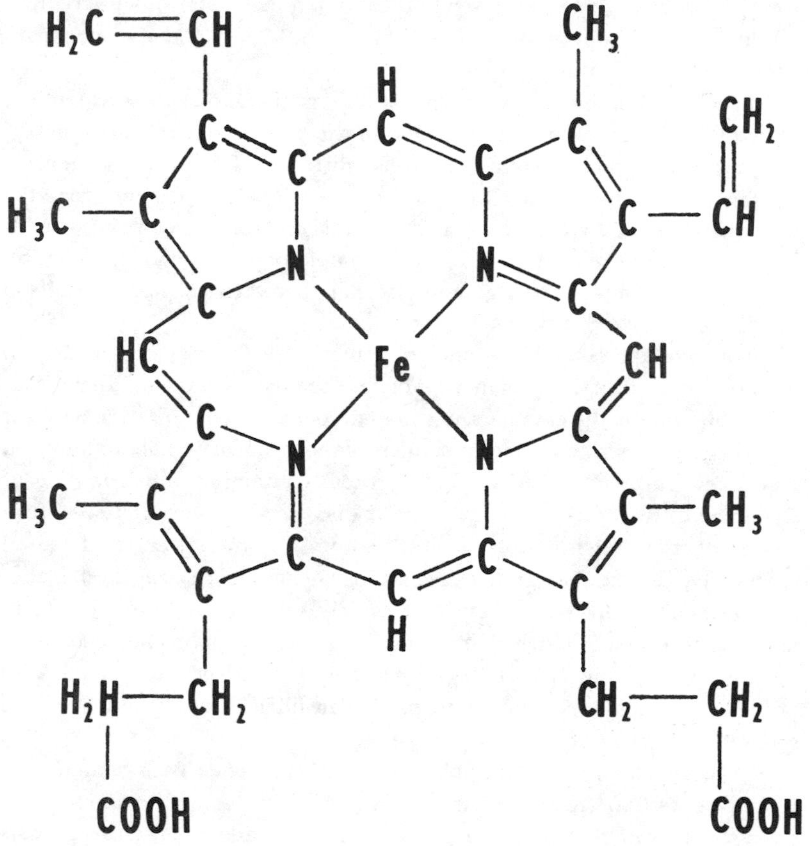

Fig. 19.   *The heme group of human hemoglobin*

carrying of oxygen, the total structure of the heme portion as well as the globin or protein portion is essential for proper hemoglobin activity.

Why are protein molecules so important to the living cell? There are several reasons for this, and one is hemoglobin activity. Among the other many roles played by proteins, perhaps the most crucial as far as the origin of life is concerned, is their role as biological catalysts or **enzymes.** Enzymes speed up chemical reactions which are essential to the life process but which would not occur at all, or else would occur at a negligible rate, under nonbiological conditions. It is conservatively estimated that a "typical" living cell contains 1,500-2,000 *different* enzymes catalyzing 1,500-2,000 *different* chemical reactions. On the average (there are exceptions), enzymes carry out their functional roles under very mild conditions of an optimum acidity range of 6.8-7.4 pH and an optimum temperature range of 98-115° F.

The nature and biological activity of any protein molecule is dependent primarily on the amino acid sequence in the protein chain. For example, the sequence—glycine-alanine-valine—is different from the sequence—glycine-valine-alanine—just as the sequence—A-B-C—is different from the sequence—A-C-B—. We have already seen that the sequence of amino acids in protein structure is crucial, and an example of this is that the substitution of two valines for two glutamic acids in human hemoglobin results in the disease known as sickle cell anemia.

If one should take the seventeen letters A through Q of the English alphabet and arrange them in all possible sequences, he would find that over 300 trillion different arrangements would be possible. Likewise, it may be demonstrated that a similar number of different amino acid sequences are possible for a simple protein containing only *one each* of seventeen different amino acids. Now if one uses only the first seventeen letters of the English alphabet but allows certain letters to be used repeatedly, the number of different arrangements increases phenomenally. In like manner, protein structure is equally variant and complicated. In fact, the situation is much more complicated with proteins because of the possibility of amino acids being either right-handed or left-handed. This property of handedness presents particular difficulties in terms of the spontaneous origin of the first living thing.

For a typical protein of only twelve amino acids with a molecular weight of 34,000 (relatively simple) where all twelve of the amino acids are used repeatedly to give a total of 288 peptide bonds, there exists approximately 10^{300} different molecules which arise due only to the alteration of the sequence of amino acids. The number 10^{300} is so large it is meaningless. However, if each molecule weighs 10^{-20} grams (much too small a weight to be detected even with the most accurate analytical balance), then the total weight of the 10^{300} molecules would be 10^{280} grams. This figure is also meaningless, but it becomes meaningful when one realizes that the total mass of the earth is only 10^{27} grams! Remember that this calculation applies to only one relatively simple protein. However, a single living cell may require 1,500-2,000 *different* such protein molecules in order to carry on the life process. Furthermore, each of the 1,500 or so different protein molecules in a living cell must be faithfully reproduced at rates absolutely inconceivable to the human mind.

Were you a chemist starting four and one-half billion years ago (presumably about when the earth was formed), you would have had to synthesize 7×10^{284} protein molecules *per second* in order to have synthesized 10^{300} molecules by the present. At the rate of synthesizing one molecule per second and starting four and one-half billion years ago, you would have synthesized far less than one billionth of one billionth of one percent of the 10^{300} molecules by the present. It is estimated that all living species in both the plant and animal kingdoms on the earth are composed of 10^{10}-10^{12} different kinds of protein molecules.

Now the materialist claims that the foregoing facts as to the infinite variety of structures among the proteins support his hypothesis of the origin of life. The idea is that **natural selection** was operative at the molecular level billions of years ago, and only those protein structures conducive to the evolution of life were selected from among the population of perhaps trillions and trillions of different protein structures. The argument is a priori; that is, it is an argument based on theory instead of experiment. Furthermore, it does not seem likely that the hypothesis could be tested since it would require trillions of protein molecules and millions of years to conduct such an experiment. The fact is that the above observations offer, at present, insuperable difficulties for mechanistic materialism. It is inconceivable that an ultrasimple, hypothetical original cell containing as few as 150 different protein enzymes and appropriate genetic material could spontaneously arise without any ordering force *extra* to the material world. However, let us assume that such an unlikely event (probability $\cong 0$) actually did occur. Before such a cell could reproduce, each of the 150 different protein enzymes must be reproduced faithfully with exact precision. One single mistake in the substitution of any one amino acid in any one of the 150 different proteins would have doubtless resulted in a fatal mutation. It is not sufficient to say simply that bacteria and alga reproduce faithfully and, therefore, the original primordial cell would also have reproduced faithfully, because the original cell is far less sophisticated in structure, organization, and function than bacteria or algae. Furthermore, the original cell would somehow have had to overcome a primeval environment totally hostile to its very existence. This aspect of the problem of the spontaneous generation of life will be considered in detail in chapter 4.

Nucleotides to Polynucleotides (Nucleic Acids)

Genetic information, such as the color of one's hair, color of one's eyes, one's height, and even many aspects of one's metabolism, is determined by giant molecules called deoxyribonucleic acid (DNA). A person receives half of his genetic material (DNA) from his mother and half from his father on a random mixing basis. His parents, in turn, received half of their DNA from each of their parents. Hence one-fourth of a person's DNA came from each of his grandparents and one-eighth from each of his great-grandparents, and so on. This genetic information that is coded into the structure of DNA is transferred to another nucleic acid, ribonucleic acid (RNA), and RNA directs the synthesis of all protein, such as enzymes, muscle, hemoglobin, and connective tissue. This important functional role

HETEROCYCLIC BASE--SUGAR--PHOSPHATE

(a)

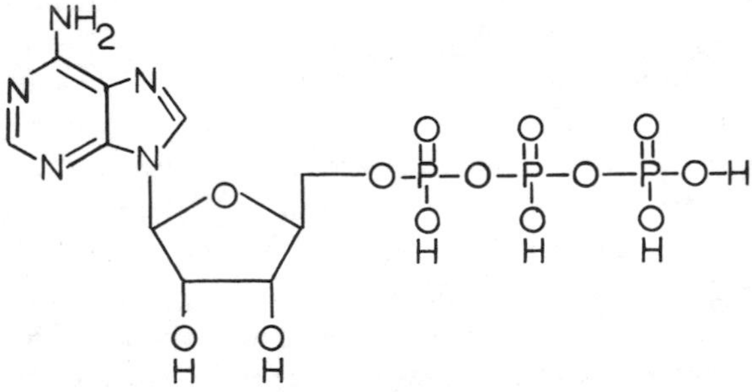

(b)

Fig. 20.   (a) composition of nucleotides and
              (b) a specific nucleotide, ATP

of DNA exists throughout the animal and plant kingdoms regardless of how simple or complex the organism.

The nucleic acids, DNA and RNA, are polymers of individual nucleotides. Nucleotides are, in turn, composed of nitrogen-containing cyclic molecules called heterocyclic bases, which are bonded to a sugar molecule (either **ribose** or **deoxyribose**), which, in turn, is bonded to a phosphate residue. Figure 20a represents the general composition of nucleotides and Figure 20b shows the structure of a specific nucleotide, adenosine triphosphate, ATP.

The heterocyclic bases in DNA are cytosine (C), adenine (A), guanine (G), and thymine (T); and in RNA one finds cytosine (C), adenine (A), guanine (G), and uracil (U). These structures are shown in Figure 21.

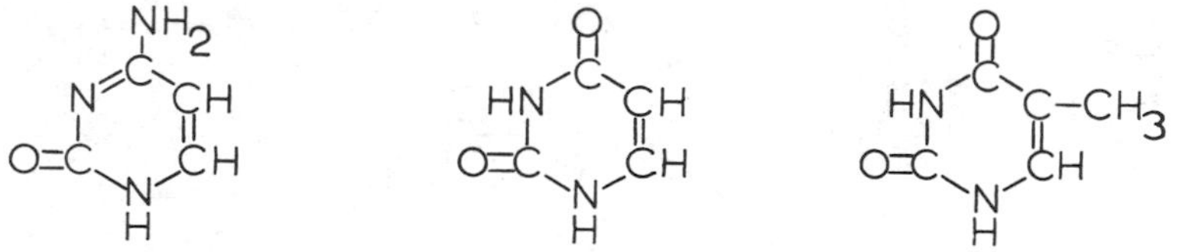

CYTOSINE (C)   URACIL (U)   THYMINE (T)

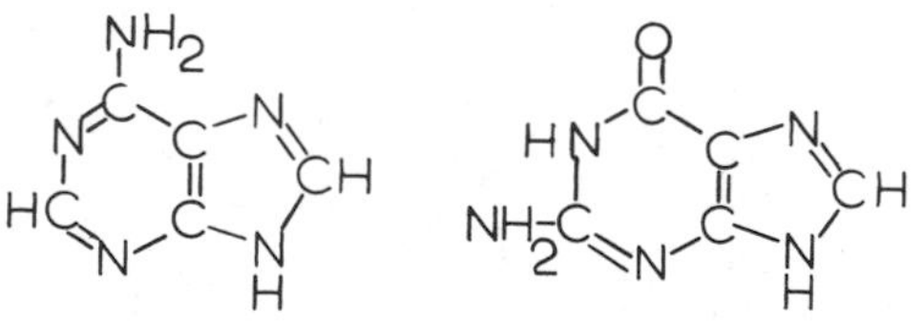

ADENINE (A)   GUANINE (G)

Fig. 21.   Heterocyclic bases found in human DNA and RNA. Some eight additional heterocyclic bases have been discovered elsewhere in plants and animals.

DNA is a double-stranded molecule and its structure is represented in Figure 22. The elucidation of this structure is recognized as one of the most significant achievements of modern science. The two strands are long chain polymers of nucleotides. The chains of nucleotides are turned together to produce a double helix. The strands are bridged across to one another by the way of intermolecular associations of the heterocyclic bases through hydrogen bonds to give an overall effect of a spiral staircase.

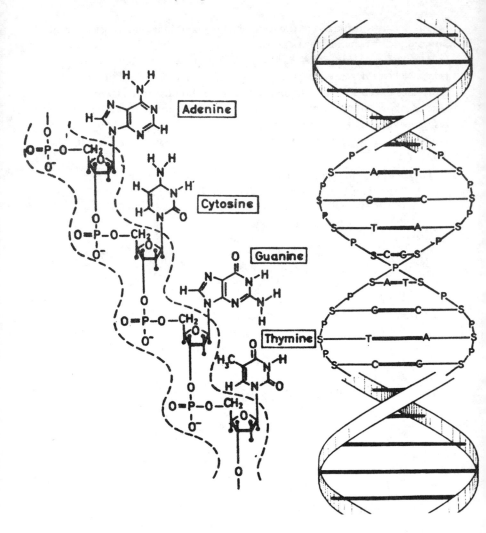

*Fig. 22   (Left) A segment of a single strand of DNA. (Right)
the double helix of DNA showing base pairing.*

The structure of RNA is similar to that of DNA except that uracil (U)
has been substituted for thymine (T) and RNA is not double stranded as is
DNA. The size of these giant molecules is staggering to the imagination.
Literally thousands of nucleotides are combined to give single DNA

molecules and in humans the linear DNA sequence is estimated to contain on the order of one billion nucleotides.[8] In a single bacterial cell of *Escherichia coli* the number of individual nucleotides in its DNA is estimated at ten million.[9] If one represented the nucleotide sequence of DNA in a single bacterial cell of *E. coli* by the letters C, A, T, and G where each letter represented one nucleotide of cytosine, adenine, thymine, and guanine respectively, then the *sequence of letters alone* would be sufficient to fill two complete volumes of the *Encyclopaedia Britannica*. A similar representation of the nucleotide sequence in the human DNA of *any one* of the trillions of cells in the human body would be sufficient to fill completely every volume of 40 sets of the *Encyclopaedia Britannica*. Suffice it to say that if the DNA of the "primordial cell" were smaller than even bacterial or viral DNA by a factor of several million, the molecule would still have been inconceivably complex.

According to current views on genetic coding, it takes DNA with a molecular weight of about 600,000 to encode for one enzyme molecule.[10] However, the original or primordial hypothetical cell would have contained a minimum of 150 different enzyme molecules, as we have already pointed out. This means that the original primordial cell would have required DNA in the amount of 150 million, if present observation can be regarded as even a rough predictor of conditions that must have prevailed earlier. This fact alone would have completely prohibited its formation by chance and probability factors alone under the ruthless conditions that must have prevailed upon the primeval earth. Furthermore, one molecule of DNA alone, regardless of how large it may have been, could not have exhibited the life principle. The original living thing as conceived by the materialist must have consisted of a rather complex combination of DNA or DNA-like substance, proteins which would have functioned as enzymes, energy-yielding substrate molecules for the primordial cell to "feed" on, and a host of inorganic ions and molecules. If the materialist would retort that it is unfair to apply observations on present living things to the original or primordial cell, then we would quickly remind him that we are

8. M. Eden, "Inadequacies of Neo-Darwinian Evolution as a Scientific Theory," in *Mathematical Challenges to the Neo-Darwinian Interpretation of Evolution*, ed. P. S. Moorhead and M. M. Kaplan (Philadelphia: The Wistar Institute Press, 1967), p. 110.

9. C. R. Woese, *The Genetic Code* (New York: Harper and Row, Publishers, 1967), p. 10.

10. J. D. Watson, *Molecular Biology of the Gene*, 2nd ed. (New York: W. A. Benjamin, Inc., 1970), p. 99.

only applying his principle of uniformitarianism to the problem of spontaneous generation. This principle maintains that processes which prevail on the earth today are identical to those processes which have always prevailed on the earth. It would appear that at this level of thought, strict uniformitarianism destroys itself.

Speculation on the Earth's Primeval Conditions

Before we can seriously evaluate the mechanistic material hypothesis for the origin of life, it is necessary to consider current thought concerning the condition of the primeval earth. It is necessary to know what the primitive conditions were before one can set up an experiment which supposedly simulates those conditions. Primeval earth conditions are generally discussed under the headings of atmosphere, radiation, and the composition of the earth's crust. In this section we are principally concerned with the earth's primitive atmosphere. Radiation or energy sources and the earth's primitive crust will be considered in chapter 4.

It is generally assumed that the earth's primeval atmosphere was a reducing one; that is, it contained hydrogen, among other things, but little, if any, oxygen. Components other than hydrogen thought to have been constituents of the primeval atmosphere are methane, nitrogen, ammonia, water, hydrogen sulfide, alkanes, and smaller amounts of carbon dioxide and carbon monoxide.[11] However, it is frequently acknowledged that we cannot be positive that the earth's primeval atmosphere was reducing. For example, S. L. Miller states near the close of one of his classic papers:

> These ideas are of course speculation, for we do not know that the Earth had a reducing atmosphere when it was formed. Most of the geological record has been altered in the four to five billion years since then, so that no direct evidence has yet been found.[12]

Melvin Calvin, a foremost authority on the mechanistic approach to the origin-of-life problem, states:

> We should try to decide what sort of earth, i.e., what sort of chemicals, we had to deal with, and what the earth was like at

11. S. L. Miller and H. C. Urey, "Organic Compound Synthesis on the Primitive Earth," *Science*, Vol. 130 (1959), pp. 245-251.
12. S. L. Miller, "Production of Some Organic Compounds Under Possible Primitive Conditions," *Journal of the American Chemical Society*, 77 (1955), p. 2351.

that time. Unfortunately, the geochemists can't agree on whether the atmosphere of the earth was an oxidized one or a reduced one, or some intermediate state between.[13]

The following are three of the reasons generally given for assuming that the earth's primitive atmosphere was a reducing one. The first two reasons are objective; the third is essentially subjective.

1. Assuming either the big-bang, expanding universe, or proto-planet hypothesis for the origin of the universe, one concludes that the earth and the remainder of the solar system condensed from a cosmic dust cloud which was rich in hydrogen. This means that the earth's original atmosphere consisted largely of hydrogen gas. However, hydrogen is the lightest of the elements; and over very long periods of time the molecules of hydrogen in the atmosphere would, by molecular collisions, gain sufficient velocity to escape the earth's gravitational field and diffuse into outer space. This velocity is known as hydrogen's escape velocity. Credulity is given to this idea by the observation that some of the planets of our solar system, such as Jupiter, Saturn, Uranus, and Neptune, still have reducing atmospheres of methane, ammonia, and hydrogen.

2. Meteorites, *assumed to be like primitive earth stuff,* are highly reduced chemically. Iron appears in meteorites as metallic iron and ferrous sulfide; carbon appears as free carbon or iron carbide; and phosphorus appears as phosphides. The gases listed above, presumably as components of the earth's primitive atmosphere, would have preserved this primeval earth chemistry until molecular oxygen appeared as an atmospheric component. Compounds inconsistent with the supposedly reduced primeval earth chemistry are—in addition to oxygen—ozone, oxides of nitrogen, and oxides of sulfur.[14]

3. It is generally (though not universally) conceded that bio-organic compounds could not have spontaneously appeared under an oxidizing atmosphere in sufficient amounts for life to have spontaneously arisen. The following are three generally recognized reasons for believing that bio-organic molecules could not have evolved on a primitive earth having an atmosphere enriched with oxygen.[15]

    a. It is observed that molecular oxygen shows a deleterious effect on many aspects of cell metabolism, and it is thought

13. M. Calvin, "Chemical Evolution and the Origin of Life," *American Scientist, 44* (1956), p. 249.
14. Miller and Urey, p. 245.
15. R. L. Lemmon, "Chemical Evolution," *Chemical Reviews, 70* (1970), p. 95.

that this inhibition due to molecular oxygen would extend to the primordial cell system. Since **anaerobic** (without oxygen) processes could not evolve in the presence of oxygen, it is concluded that the initial bio-organics were formed in the absence of oxygen; that is, a reducing atmosphere. One recognizes that this order of reasoning is in keeping with the principle of uniformitarianism to which we recently alluded.

b. Certain aspects of the biochemistry of chromosomes and cell division are known to require anaerobic conditions. Again, the principle of uniformity suggests that this fact would extend to the primordial cell system. It is claimed that life, as we know it, could not have evolved under **aerobic** (with oxygen) conditions and hence the conclusion that bio-organics were formed under anaerobic conditions.

c. Third, it is observed that many experiments designed to synthesize bio-organic compounds under simulated primordial conditions fail in the presence of molecular oxygen but produce bio-organics in the absence of oxygen. One reason for this is that molecular oxygen effectively inhibits certain types of chemical reactions such as free-radical processes. Hence, bio-organic-producing free-radical reactions would have been essentially eliminated if aerobic conditions had prevailed on the primordial earth.

Yet, *here we are;* and the materialist insists that we must have evolved spontaneously from inorganic matter. Hence it follows that the materialist must conclude that the earth's primeval atmosphere was a reducing one and not an oxidizing one, since it does not seem possible that life could have evolved under oxidizing conditions. The reasoning here seems to follow this course:

Presupposition:	Matter is the only eternal principle.
Observation:	Here we are.
Conclusion:	Life evolved from inorganic matter.
Observation:	Pre-life materials could not have originated in an oxidizing atmosphere.
Conclusion:	Earth's primeval atmosphere was reducing.

The validity of either conclusion depends on the validity of the original presupposition. As stated in chapter 1, it is inherently impossible to demonstrate the validity of this statement; we can only examine the evidence that tends to support or deny its validity. Thus far, the evidence tends to deny the validity of the presupposition as far as the origin-of-life problem is concerned.

Finally, it should be sufficient to state that if we do not know (and cannot know for certain) what the primitive earth conditions were, then we should not expect to be able to simulate those conditions in a modern laboratory. *We cannot simulate what we do not know.* Furthermore, any conclusion deduced from experiments performed under such simulated primitive earth conditions can at best only be regarded as tentative and conditional.

CHAPTER 4

A CRITIQUE OF THE THREE-STAGE MECHANISTIC HYPOTHESIS OF THE ORIGIN OF LIFE

Introduction

Two points have been emphasized in this text: (1) the problem of origins is basically philosophical, and (2) even the simplest life forms are so immensely complex as to virtually eliminate the possibility of the spontaneous formation of life. Furthermore, we have seen that our knowledge of the conditions of the primeval earth is essentially speculative. There is no objection to a mechanistic hypothesis of origins as long as the philosophical, metaphysical, and theological aspects of the problem are not ignored and as long as a hypothesis is not elevated to the status of fact. We do not intend to imply that every scientist interested in the origin-of-life problem should simply say "God did it" and then cease further experimentation bearing on the problem of how life *could* have originated on earth. The fact is, however, that current leading authorities in this area of thought either completely ignore or repudiate the theological alternative. We would simply recommend that it be recognized by all concerned that mechanistic materialism is indeed a philosophical concept and, if this philosophy is to be given consideration, then the philosophical, theological view should not be ignored. We are not so much concerned that every scientist accept the theological view (for it is impractical to expect that this could occur); we merely want it to be recognized that there is a logical alternative to mechanistic materialism. We will now examine the three-stage hypothesis of origins as is generally visualized by those professing mechanistic materialism.

The Three-Stage Hypothesis of the Origin of Life

The three-stage hypothesis of the origin of life summarized in Figure 23 is that which is generally suggested by the mechanistic materialist. Stage One consists of the spontaneous origin of bio-organic molecules from

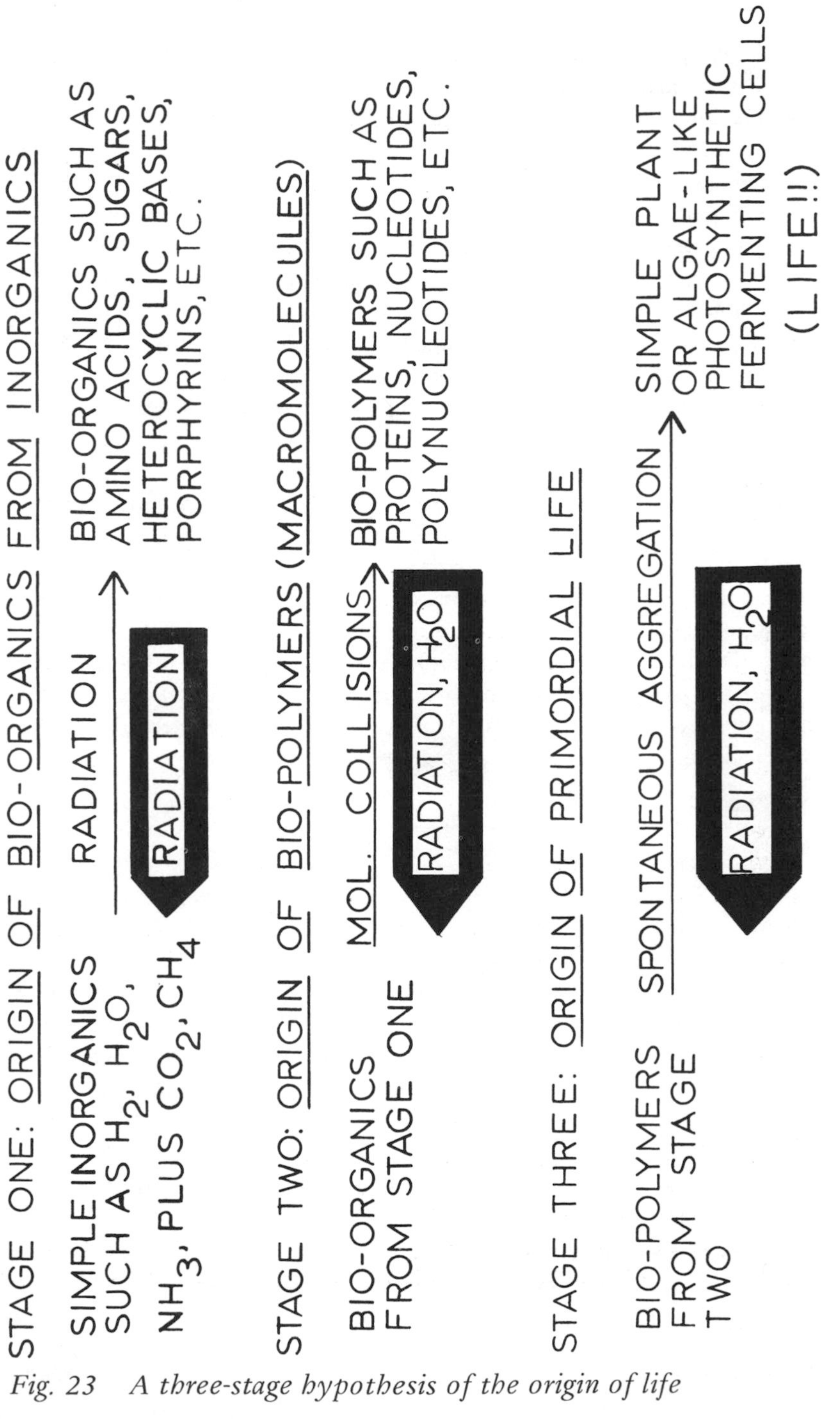

STAGE ONE: ORIGIN OF BIO-ORGANICS FROM INORGANICS

SIMPLE INORGANICS
SUCH AS H_2, H_2O,
NH_3, PLUS CO_2, CH_4

RADIATION
$\xrightarrow{\text{RADIATION}}$

BIO-ORGANICS SUCH AS
AMINO ACIDS, SUGARS,
HETEROCYCLIC BASES,
PORPHYRINS, ETC.

STAGE TWO: ORIGIN OF BIO-POLYMERS (MACROMOLECULES)

BIO-ORGANICS
FROM STAGE ONE

MOL. COLLISIONS
$\xrightarrow{\text{RADIATION, } H_2O}$

BIO-POLYMERS SUCH AS
PROTEINS, NUCLEOTIDES,
POLYNUCLEOTIDES, ETC.

STAGE THREE: ORIGIN OF PRIMORDIAL LIFE

BIO-POLYMERS
FROM STAGE
TWO

SPONTANEOUS AGGREGATION
$\xrightarrow{\text{RADIATION, } H_2O}$

SIMPLE PLANT
OR ALGAE-LIKE
PHOTOSYNTHETIC
FERMENTING CELLS
(LIFE!!)

Fig. 23   *A three-stage hypothesis of the origin of life*

simple inorganic matter and the earth's primeval reducing atmosphere, which presumably consisted of hydrogen gas, water, ammonia, carbon dioxide, and methane. From the bio-organics produced in Stage One it is postulated that in Stage Two bio-polymers, such as proteins and polynucleotides, arose due to some yet unknown ordering principle. Finally, in Stage Three, it is suggested that a spontaneous aggregation of the bio-polymers from Stage Two resulted in the evolution of primordial life which is generally thought to have been simple plant, **algae**like, fermenting cells. However, there is no unanimity of opinion as to the exact nature of the first living things. The spontaneous generation of life from inorganic terrestrial matter is called **abiogenesis.**

There is also proposed a fourth stage, which is really life evolving from life or **biogenesis.** This stage is illustrated in Figure 24. The photosynthetic, fermenting, algaelike plants presumably formed in Stage One are thought to have fed off the carbon dioxide in the primitive earth's reducing atmosphere. These photosynthetic, fermenting, algaelike plants would have produced oxygen and carbohydrates as by-products of their metabolism. Since our present atmosphere is oxidizing (contains oxygen), it is postulated that the first photosynthetic life forms evolved into respiring land life, which then would have begun to feed off the oxygen and carbohydrates produced by the first primitive organisms. Eventually, it is supposed that a "balance of nature" developed between the photosynthetic organisms and the respiring land organisms.

PHOTOSYNTHETIC AQUEOUS LIFE $\longrightarrow$ $\longleftarrow$ RESPIRING LAND LIFE

$$CO_2 + H_2O \rightleftarrows (CH_2O)_n + O_2 \qquad (CH_2O)_n + O_2 \rightleftarrows nCO_2 + H_2O$$

Fig. 24.   A proposed fourth stage in the origin of life

The foregoing is a very general overview of the materialistic hypothesis of the origin of life. We will now examine the first three stages of the hypothesis. The design of this discussion is to evaluate the hypothesis objectively and fairly. We will concentrate on its strengths, weaknesses, and presuppositions.

Stage One: Origin of Bio-organics from Inorganics

It is at Stage One that the greatest amount of experimental success has been achieved in an attempt to duplicate in the laboratory those **pre-biotic**

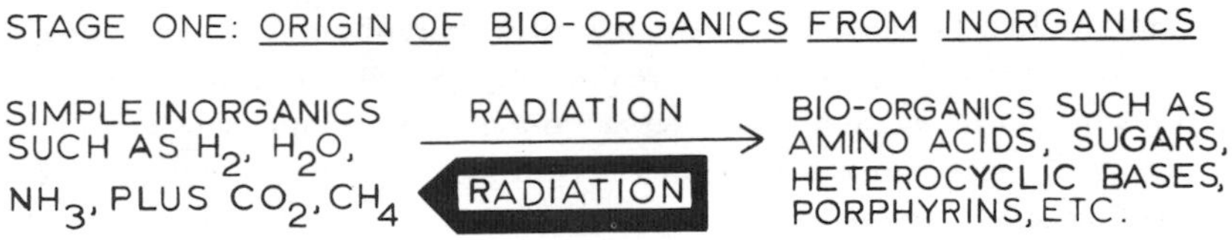

STAGE ONE: ORIGIN OF BIO-ORGANICS FROM INORGANICS

SIMPLE INORGANICS
SUCH AS H_2, H_2O,
NH_3, PLUS CO_2, CH_4

RADIATION
————————→
◀ **RADIATION**

BIO-ORGANICS SUCH AS
AMINO ACIDS, SUGARS,
HETEROCYCLIC BASES,
PORPHYRINS, ETC.

Fig. 25.   Stage One of the origin-of-life hypothesis

processes thought to have eventually produced a living thing. Some very brilliant and ingenious laboratory research has been carried out in this area. The assumptions on which these carefully designed laboratory experiments are based are generally the following:

1. The earth's primeval atmosphere was a reducing one and consisted principally of hydrogen, methane, water, ammonia, and carbon dioxide.

2. Primeval energy sources were one or a combination of the following, which are listed in the order of suspected *decreasing* importance:

   a. ultraviolet radiation from the sun
   b. lightning and corona electrical discharges
   c. cosmic rays
   d. radioactive disintegration
   e. volcanic energy and hot springs

3. Synthesis forces were overall more effective than degradation or dissolution forces. (This assumption appears to be the weakest of the three assumptions. The reasons for this will be discussed below under "dissolution.")

The literature abounds in reports on the synthesis of bio-organics under simulated pre-biotic conditions. One of the classic experiments on the synthesis of bio-organics under simulated pre-biotic conditions was performed by S. L. Miller at the University of Chicago in 1955.[1] Miller passed a continuous seven-day electric discharge through a closed system (see Fig. 26) containing methane, ammonia, water, and hydrogen. Analysis of the

1. S. L. Miller, "Production of Some Organic Compounds Under Possible Primitive Earth Conditions," *Journal of the American Chemical Society*, 77 (1955), p. 2351.

concentrated products by paper chromatography showed the formation of several amino acids and other related compounds. The syntheses were shown not to be due to bacterial contamination, and substitution of nitrogen for ammonia only changed yield ratios. Miller's results have been confirmed by other workers.[2]

A drawing of Miller's apparatus is shown in Figure 26. The apparatus was so designed that products formed at the spark gap would settle in the small spherical section in the lower part of the apparatus. Consequently, products formed were not subject to decomposition by radiation at the spark gap due to recycling in the *closed* system. Under the primeval conditions of an *open* system, however, compounds formed in the atmosphere by lightning or ultraviolet discharges would have been subject to decomposition by the same radiation effects that produced them until the products fell to the earth and settled to a depth of about ten meters below the ocean surface. Only by assuming the presence, in large quanti-

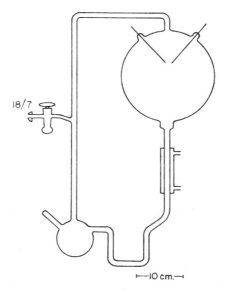

18/7

⊢—10 cm.—⊣

Fig. 26.   The Miller apparatus

ties, of a unique atmospheric component, such as hydrogen sulfide, is it conceivable that primitive amino acid molecules would not have been destroyed by radiation before reaching the earth's primeval waters. The

2. P. H. Abelson, *Science,* 124 (1956), p. 935.

hydrogen sulfide could have absorbed radiation harmful to the fragile amino acid molecules.[3] More will be said later about this decomposition or dissolution effect. Products settling on land masses were doomed to certain destruction by the same radiation effects that formed them.

Porphyrins have been obtained by passing electric discharges through ammonia, methane, and water. One of these investigators states:

> If our conclusions are right, then we have hit on a route to porphyrin genesis that might have taken place under conditions that very likely prevailed on this planet billions of years ago.[4]

One can profitably note the caution with which the above statement was made.

Adenine, a **heterocyclic base,** is formed by the **polymerization** of anhydrous hydrogen cyanide in liquid ammonia[5] in fifteen percent yield. Adenine is also known to arise from the polymerization of aqueous hydrogen cyanide in ammonia, although the yield was only 0.3–0.5 percent.[6]

Certain sugars have also been obtained under conditions thought to simulate pre-biotic earth conditions. For example, scientists at the National Aeronautics and Space Administration Ames Research Center, Moffett Field, California, refluxed dilute (0.02 and 0.33 molar) aqueous solutions of formaldehyde with alumina on either of two naturally occurring aluminosilicates, kaolinite and illite, and observed the formation of significant amounts of **triose, tetrose, pentose,** and **hexose** sugars.[7] Among the pentoses were found **ribose,** essential for the polynucleotide ribonucleic acid (RNA) and **deoxyribose,** essential for the polynucleotide deoxyribonucleic acid (DNA). Many additional investigators have experienced success in obtaining simple bio-organic chemicals under simulated pre-biotic conditions.[8]

3. C. Sagen and B. N. Khare, "Long-Wavelength Ultraviolet Photoproduction of Amino Acids on the Primitive Earth," *Science,* 173 (1971), p. 417.

4. *Chemical and Engineering News,* 6 November 1967, p. 20.

5. H. Wakamatsu, Y. Yamada, T. Saito, I. Kumashiro, and T. Takenishi, "Synthesis of Adenine by Oligomerization of Hydrogen Cyanide," *Journal of Organic Chemistry, 31* (1966), p. 2035.

6. J. Oro and A. P. Kimball, "Synthesis of Purines Under Possible Primitive Earth Conditions. I. Adenine from Hydrogen Cyanide," *Arch. Biochem. Biophys.,* (1961), p. 217.

7. *Chemical and Engineering News,* 18 September 1967, p. 53.

8. J. E. Pulliam and F. Long, *Irreversible Thermodynamics and the Origin of Life, an Annotated Bibliography* (George Washington University Medical Center, 1969), 671 references.

In concluding our comments on Stage One, it is recognized that controlled laboratory experiments have definitely shown that, under suitable simulated pre-biotic conditions and with proper starting materials, a wide variety of bio-organic molecules have been synthesized in the laboratory.

Furthermore, these synthetic chemicals are in all respects identical to bio-organic chemicals which serve as the building blocks of life as we know and understand it today. In all instances there are three agents involved in these experiments. These agents are (1) availability of starting materials, (2) the selection and use of a suitable energy source, and (3) an ordering intelligence which carried out the experiment in a *closed system.*

Now let us contrast the above agents which are present in a modern experiment under simulated pre-biotic conditions with the analogous agents which mechanistic materialism maintains prevailed on the primitive earth during the "original experiment." These agents are (1) availability of starting materials (chap. 1 shows that mechanistic materialism cannot satisfactorily account for this), (2) the right amount of the right kind of energy (neither can mechanistic materialism offer a suitable explanation for the ultimate energy source), and (3) perfect randomness (no intelligence) operating in an *open system.*

There is no question that bio-organic precursors to life spontaneously arise when the appropriate *starting materials,* in the *right amounts,* are brought together under the *right conditions* of the *proper amount* of the *right kind of energy.* However, it seems to be a blatant denial of logic to suppose that although an ordering intelligence is necessary to bring these variables together in a closed system, a similar ordering intelligence would not be necessary in an open system. We do not deny that the biochemical precursors of life would have arisen spontaneously if this happy combination of factors just happened to exist on the primitive earth. The really big question, though, is, "If this combination of factors existed at all, did it just happen to exist?" We think not. The conditions that led to the emergence of life on earth were not just a grand coincidence. Rather, the earth was deliberately prepared for the creation of life by God Himself.

Stage Two: Origin of Bio-polymers (Macromolecules)

The materialist proposes that the chance interaction of bio-organic molecules in keeping with the laws of physics and chemistry resulted in the synthesis of bio-polymers, such as proteins and nucleotides. This is held to be true because it is maintained that the same laws governing

STAGE TWO: <u>ORIGIN OF BIO-POLYMERS (MACROMOLECULES)</u>

BIO-ORGANICS   MOL. COLLISIONS   BIO-POLYMERS SUCH AS
FROM STAGE ONE   PROTEINS, NUCLEOTIDES,
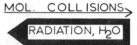 POLYNUCLEOTIDES, ETC.

Fig. 27. Stage Two of the origin-of-life hypothesis

chemical reactions today must have been operative billions of years ago. It is, therefore, appropriate to present a brief discussion of the major factors known to govern chemical reactions and rate processes.

Requirements for Productive Chemical Reactions

The student of chemistry recognizes that certain basic requirements must be met before random molecular collisions are productive. These basic requirements involve either a transfer of energy (thermodynamics) or the rate at which transformations occur (kinetics). An in-depth treatment of chemical thermodynamics and chemical kinetics is beyond the intent of this text. However, a brief comment on each is essential before one can begin to understand Stage Two of the origin-of-life hypothesis.

a. Thermodynamics

The observant reader can easily see the relevance of the three laws of thermodynamics to the origin-of-life problem. These laws may be stated as follows:

First Law: "Energy cannot be created nor destroyed but it can be transformed from one form into another." In other words, the total amount of energy in the universe is constant; but heat energy, for example, may be converted into light energy, or potential energy (water behind a dam) may be converted into kinetic energy (water falling over a spillway).

Second Law: "Processes which occur spontaneously are those processes where interacting components tend to become more disorganized." The concept of disorder is called "entropy." For example, when an automobile tire is punctured, the somewhat ordered air molecules inside the tire spontaneously (freely and without constraint) leave the tire and become more disorganized by random motion outside the tire. Never does one find a system moving from a state of disorder to a state of order unless work is done on the system, such as pumping air into the tire.

The application of the second law of thermodynamics to the biological system is more difficult to visualize. An analogy to a mechanical system is difficult to make without the introduction of some error. As a tree (or child) grows, work is done in the biological system at the molecular level, principally through the medium of enzymes. Consequently, the biological system becomes more and more organized. During this process, the energy of the sun is converted to order within the biological system as the sun increases in disorder. Late in life and at death, spontaneous disordering occurs until finally decay results. Energy that is either borrowed from the environment to produce order or that is liberated to the environment during disordering is called *free energy*. A process in which free energy is given up to the environment is called a "spontaneous" process.

The relevance of the second law of thermodynamics to the origin-of-life problem is immediately apparent. It is argued by mechanistic materialists that matter freely and without constraint became more and more organized until finally life resulted (see Fig. 9). Furthermore, it is maintained that this process of the original trapping and conservation of free energy occurred independently of an ordering intelligence.

No single step in the mechanistic approach to the origin-of-life problem is thermodynamically impossible as far as is presently known. Any chemical reaction or sequence of reactions is thermodynamically possible if it results *overall* in free energy being returned to the environment by the reacting molecules. The thermodynamic problem, as far as the origin of life is concerned, is simply this: "How did the mechanism for the spontaneous ordering of molecules arise?" In other words, "How was the original conversion of energy to order done in the complete absence of a system designed to make the conversion?" The mechanistic materialists argue that the system which resulted in the conversion of energy to order was inherent within matter itself, but this is an argument *after the experiment*. The validity of the argument depends totally on the validity of the mechanistic material presupposition that *matter is the only eternal principle*.

Another important aspect of thermodynamic considerations is the concept of equilibrium. Consider molecules A and B reacting to give products C and D. This reaction is expressed as follows:

$$A + B \rightleftharpoons C + D$$

This reaction will continue to give additional quantities of products C and D as long as the reaction results in free energy being released to the environment. No more build-up of products C and D will occur once the change in free energy of the reaction equals zero. At this point we say that the system has "attained equilibrium." Of utmost importance for our purposes here is the fact that the concentrations of products C and D need not be equal to the concentration of the reactants, A and B, once equilibrium has been attained ($\Delta F = 0$). The concentrations of C and D may be either much greater than A and B or much less than A and B. We say that if the equilibrium constant for the reaction is 10^{-3} (0.001), then *at equilibrium* there exists 1,000 times more A and B than C and D. On the other hand, if the equilibrium constant for the reaction is 10^2 (100), then there will be 100 times more C and D at equilibrium than A and B. We will shortly return to this most important concept of chemical equilibrium.

The second law of thermodynamics may be paraphrased by saying that the universe is spontaneously tending toward greater disorder or that the universe is similar to a clock that is running down. This statement of the second law, of course, implies that the universe at one time had to be set in motion (wound up), which is perfectly consistent with the creationist view.

Third Law: "Perfect order is attained only in a perfect crystal at absolute zero temperature." This law has little relevance to our present discussion.

b. Kinetics

The study of the rates of chemical reactions is called chemical kinetics. By "rate" one simply means the number of molecules of products which are formed per unit of time. Time may be measured in any convenient unit such as seconds, hours, years, or even billions of years. The overall rate, or how fast a reaction occurs, may be expressed by the following equation which, as is easily seen, contains a number of variables:

| Rate = | Frequency of molecular collisions | x | Fraction of collisions that have sufficient energy to react | x | Fraction of molecules that have sufficient energy to react which are properly oriented upon collision. |

The first factor—frequency of molecular collisions—depends on three principal variables. They are:

1. The concentration of reacting molecules. It is apparent that the closer molecules are together, the more likely they are to collide.

2. The size of the reacting molecules. It is also apparent that large molecules will collide more frequently than small molecules, provided other conditions are equal.

3. The speed with which the molecules move about. Rapidly moving molecules will tend to collide more frequently than slowly moving molecules as long as other conditions are equal. The speed at which molecules move depends on two additional variables. These variables are:

  a. The masses of the reacting molecules. Heavy molecules tend to move slower than small ones, just as a small person can normally move more freely than a large person.

  b. The temperature of the environment. At higher temperatures molecules have greater internal energies and upon collision they rebound with increased vigor. Hence, their average velocities are increased.

The second factor—energy—in the above equation depends on two variables. These are:

1. The temperature of the environment (see "b" above).

2. The energy of activation, which is a characteristic property of each individual reaction. The energy of activation may be thought of as the minimal amount of collision energy necessary to cause a chemical reaction to take place.

The third factor—orientation—in the above equation also depends on two variables, which are:

1. The geometry of the reacting molecules. Normally a chemical reaction will occur at only one localized site within a molecule, and the colliding molecules must collide at that site before a productive reaction occurs. Due to the shape or geometry of a molecule, this reactive site may be so protected or "covered up" that the approach of a colliding molecule to the reactive site may be hindered. Hence, the reaction occurs only with great difficulty.

2. The kind of reaction that is taking place. Due to features of molecular structure, some molecules are simply not candidates for reaction of a particular type. Thus unlimited collisions of molecules in this case do not result in the formation of any product at all.

But what does all of this have to do with the origin-of-life problem? Simply this: In order for a chemical reaction to occur at an optimal rate, all of the above variables must be carefully regulated. Too much of one variable or too little of another variable may result in a great reduction in the time required for sufficient quantities of an intermediate to build up. The mechanistic hypothesis maintains that all variables and conditions necessary for the spontaneous origin of life were met by random or chance factors alone. Again, we insist that this is an argument *after the experiment,* and its validity depends totally on the validity of the materialistic presupposition which was discussed in chapter 1.

The Time Factor in the Spontaneous Generation of Life

Clearly, these considerations of thermodynamics and kinetics have brought us to the question of the time factor involved in the origin of life. How much time would be required for life to spontaneously evolve? Or, is there any likelihood at all that such an event would occur even given indefinite time?

As pointed out earlier, there is no reason to believe that any single step in the mechanistic hypothesis of spontaneous generation of Stage Two chemicals is thermodynamically impossible. That is, *given enough time the reactions should occur, provided conditions are adequate and provided intermediates along the reaction path are sufficiently stable under existing conditions.* All of these conditions are crucial. The stability of intermediates becomes a particularly critical factor, as we will soon see. If an intermediate is unstable, it will tend to decompose before it has a chance to reach a concentration sufficient to allow the sequence to proceed to the next step in the reaction sequence. The consequence is that longer and longer periods of time are required for even minor progress to be made along a reaction path, unless conditions are continually optimal. In the pages to follow we will see that there is an ever diminishing likelihood that even billions of years are sufficiently long for the spontaneous generation of life to occur from inorganic chemicals under the sterile and ruthless conditions of the primitive earth. However, we cannot authoritatively and dogmatically say that two billion years was *not* enough time for life to spontaneously evolve; but we surely cannot be so presumptuous as to say that it *was* enough time. J. D. Bernal states: "The basic defect of mechanistic explanations in biology is that they effectively ignore the time factor."[9] Melvin Calvin, Nobel Prize winner and champion of chemical evolution, states:

9. J. D. Bernal, *The Origin of Life* (New York: Universe Books, Publisher, 1967), p. 172.

We have plenty of time to do this—2½ billion years. Although every one of the processes that I have described is probable—there is no great improbable event that I have required—the selection amongst the random probable events of a particular sequence is a highly improbable thing and has required the billion years or so that it took to do it. And that is why I doubt very much that we will ever be able to put all the chemicals in a pot and place it in a radiation field and go away and leave it for a while and come back and find nucleic acids.[10]

There is no unanimity of opinion among researchers on the origin-of-life problem as to the percentage of all evolutionary time that was required for life to evolve on earth. Most writers agree in terms of 4.8 billion years of total evolutionary time, with the first 1.7 billion years being required for the initial life form to appear. Subsequently, another 2.5 billion years were required for the initial life form to evolve into a multicellular organism. In other words, 4.2 billion years out of a total possible 4.8 billion years are thought to be necessary for simple multicellular organisms to arise from inorganic materials by spontaneous processes.[11] The materialist is faced with an enigma that is at least presently insurmountable: ninety percent of all evolutionary time was required for a multicellular organism to spontaneously arise, yet only ten percent of all evolutionary time was required for man to spontaneously evolve from the multicellular organism! The development of man from later vertebrates is regarded by evolutionists to be a process that has occurred during the last two million years or so, which in the history of the earth is comparable to the last thirty seconds of a twenty-four-hour day.[12] This is equal to only 0.04 percent of all available evolutionary time. Molecules in collision is the *only force* within nature that the materialist invokes as being responsible for *all* biochemical, physiological, and morphological changes in life systems from inorganic chemicals to man. It is no wonder that in 1966 mathematicians at the Wistar Institute of Anatomy and Biology challenged the neo-Darwinian interpretation of evolution and the origin of life.[13]

10. M. Calvin, "Chemical Evolution and the Origin of Life," *American Scientist, 44* (1956), p. 262.
11. See Figure 34-1 in chapter "The Origin of Life," A. L. Lehninger, *Biochemistry* (New York: Worth Publishing, Inc., 1970), p. 770.
12. Lehninger, p. 771.
13. P. S. Moorhead and M. M. Kaplan, eds., *Mathematical Challenges to the Neo-Darwinian Interpretation of Evolution* (Philadelphia: The Wistar Institute Press, 1967).

As we have seen, it is supposed by the materialists that random energetic collisions of bio-organic molecules formed in Stage One led to the formation of bio-polymers and polynucleotides in Stage Two. Let us now examine the assumptions inherent within Stage Two. First, it is assumed that the right amount of the right kind of energy was available. For example, too much heat energy (around the boiling point of water and above) would have been destructive to the fragile bio-polymers; and too little heat energy (around the freezing point of water) would have meant that not enough energy was available for effective molecular collisions. Second, it is assumed that the rate of dissolution or decomposition of the newly formed bio-polymers did not greatly exceed their rate of formation. As we will soon see, this is a most formidable assumption inasmuch as both proteins and polynucleotides tend to spontaneously decay to their respective amino acids and nucleotide monomer units in the presence of water. Third, it is assumed that approximately one billion years of Stage-One processes was ample time to provide concentrations of bio-organics sufficient for the spontaneous formation of bio-polymers. Fourth, it is assumed that there was some mechanism by which order was introduced into the bio-polymer structures. For example, J. D. Bernal comments:

> I have stated and discussed the essential problem of the origin of life which, as seen now in the light of molecular biology, is: at what stage was order introduced into polymer chains? Unfortunately, it cannot be said that this problem has been solved as well as it has been stated. Put into quasi-mathematical form, as we are now forced to put it, it has indeed been shown to be much more difficult than had previously been imagined.[14]

The philosophical and practical problem of the existence of an "ordering principle" in nature is one which causes the materialist no small concern. A. L. Lehninger of the department of biochemistry at Johns Hopkins University states:

> But perhaps the most crucial stage in chemical evolution may be that point at which self-organization of organic matter first appeared, so that a specific set or cluster of different types of organic molecules was better able to survive as a group than singly. It is this last stage that is most difficult for us to

14. Bernal, p. 75.

comprehend and study, since there are very few familiar molecular prototypes of self-organizing systems.[15]

Melvin Calvin[16] has pointed out that a certain amount of spontaneous ordering of purines and pyrimidines, which are essential components of ribonucleic acid (RNA) and deoxyribonucleic acid (DNA), has been observed in solutions as dilute as 10^{-4} molar in concentration. The ordering of the purines and pyrimidines which Calvin observed is essentially like that which exists in native RNA and DNA structure. However, it is unreal to assume that large segments of DNA and RNA would spontaneously form from a pool of nucleotides merely because their constituent heterocyclic bases tend to associate in solution. Additional research needs to be done in this area.

In addition to the inability of mechanistic materialism to offer a satisfactory explanation for the spontaneous self-organization of bio-organics to give bio-polymers, there exists another problem in Stage Two that is equally formidable. This is the problem of dissolution or decomposition of the bio-polymers under the same conditions that they were supposedly formed. This is our next topic for discussion.

Concentration of Bio-organics and Macromolecules—Dissolution

In Figure 23, which shows the three-stage hypothesis of the spontaneous generation of life, we have indicated by large arrows that decomposition or dissolution of products tends to occur more rapidly than the synthesis of products. In other words, products tend to decay faster than they are formed. This is recognized by many as being the most formidable problem of spontaneous generation. George Wald is to be commended for his forthright recognition of the problem:

> In the vast majority of the processes in which we are interested the point of equilibrium lies far over toward the side of dissolution. That is to say, spontaneous dissolution is much more probable, and hence proceeds much more rapidly, than spontaneous synthesis.[17]

15. Lehninger, p. 772.
16. Calvin, p. 258.
17. G. Wald, "The Origin of Life," in *The Molecular Basis of Life*, ed. R. H. Haynes and P. C. Hanawalt (San Francisco: W. H. Freeman and Co., n.d.), p. 342.

Wald continues by observing that in a very short period of time dissolution or decay forces could undo the results of long periods of synthesis activity:

> The situation we must face is that of a patient Penelope waiting for Odysseus, yet much worse: each night she undid the weaving of the preceding day, but here a night could readily undo the work of a year or a century.[18]

Wald continues to comment to the effect that dissolution or decay of crucial chemical intermediates is the most difficult problem of spontaneous generation:

> I believe this to be the most stubborn problem that confronts us—the weakest link at present in our argument. I do not think it by any means disastrous, but it calls for phenomena and forces some of which are as yet only partly understood and some probably still to be discovered.[19]

A major reason for the above statements is that those conditions which must be assumed as necessary for the synthesis of bio-organics and macromolecules are even more effective in decomposing them. For example, ultraviolet radiation is assumed as a primary energy source for the synthesis of bio-organics; but ultraviolet radiation also causes a cleavage of the bonds of carbon compounds, leading to their decomposition.

It is possible for life to exist on earth because there is a layer of ozone in the upper reaches of our atmosphere which filters out harmful antibiotic ultraviolet radiation. This ozone is produced from atmospheric oxygen, as seen in Figure 28. Now it is supposed that the earth's primitive atmosphere contained no oxygen; hence it could have contained no ozone. No ozone would have meant that there was no antibiotic ultraviolet radiation filter in the earth's primeval atmosphere, and no ultraviolet radiation filter would certainly have made it impossible for life to have evolved near the earth's surface. The problem reduces to this: How could life have arisen in the presence of a flux of antibiotic radiation? The answer is: It could not have arisen. It seems that the only way that the mechanistic materialist has to survive this vicious cycle is to suppose that bio-organics would necessarily have been synthesized in the stratosphere, fallen to the earth's oceans before decomposition by radiation, and then

18. Wald.
19. Wald, p. 343.

$$3O_2 + \text{light} \rightleftharpoons 2O_3$$

OXYGEN   OZONE

Fig. 28.   The formation of ozone from oxygen

settled to a level of ten meters in the oceans before they would have finally been safe from decomposition by harmful radiation. The following quotation evidences to the validity of the above remarks:

> In the upper atmosphere, however, a layer of ozone, at a height of 22 to 25 kilometers, begins to absorb the sun's radiation strongly at 320 millimicrons, and at 290 millimicrons forms a virtually opaque screen. It is only the presence of this layer of ozone, removing short-wave antibiotic radiation, that makes terrestrial life possible.[20]

If amino acids were generated in the earth's upper atmosphere by radiation forces but were also subject to decomposition by those same radiation forces, then a very intriguing question is: Was the rate of decomposition of the amino acids in the atmosphere greater than or less than their rate of formation? S. L. Miller and H. C. Urey verbalize this problem as follows:

> Although it is probable, it is not certain that the large amount of energy from ultraviolet light would have made the principle contribution to the synthesis of organic compounds. Most of the photochemical reactions at these low wavelengths would have taken place in the upper atmosphere. The compounds so formed would have absorbed at longer wavelengths and there-fore might have been decomposed by this ultraviolet light before reaching the oceans. The question is whether the rate of decomposition in the atmosphere was greater or less than the rate of transport to the oceans.[21]

An attempt has been made to answer Miller and Urey's question quantitatively. At this point, the reader would do well to refer again to

20. G. Wald, "Life and Light," *Scientific American, 201,* No. 4 (October 1959), p. 94.
21. S. L. Miller and H. C. Urey, "Organic Compound Synthesis on the Primitive Earth," *Science, 130* (1959), p. 247.

Figure 25, where it is suggested by the large heavy arrow that decomposition or dissolution forces were more effective than synthesis forces. The problem stated above by Miller and Urey lends itself to quantitative calculation. This quantitative calculation was done by D. E. Hull of the California Research Corporation, who assumed the earth's primordial conditions as proposed by Miller and Urey.[22] Hull then proceeded to calculate the equilibrium constant for the formation of the amino acid **glycine** according to the following equation, which is presumably how glycine would have been formed in the earth's primeval atmosphere. Had the equilibrium constant for this reaction been 1, then at equilibrium there

$$2CH_4 \quad + \quad NH_3 \quad + \quad 2H_2 \rightleftharpoons NH_2-CH_2-COOH \quad + \quad 5H_2$$

Methane   Ammonia   Hydrogen   Glycine   Hydrogen

would have existed almost the same amount of products (glycine and hydrogen) as reactants (methane, ammonia, and hydrogen). An equilibrium constant of 100 would have meant approximately 100 times more products than reactants at equilibrium, and an equilibrium constant of 10^{-2} would have meant approximately 100 times less products than reactants at equilibrium. Hull's calculation showed an equilibrium constant of 2×10^{-40} for the reaction, which means that infinitesimal amounts of product glycine exist at equilibrium in relation to the amount of reactants. In other words, at equilibrium there would be 2 followed by 39 zeros more reactants than products! The rate of decomposition of glycine greatly exceeds its rate of formation under these assumed conditions.

Further assuming conditions imposed by Miller and Urey, Hull calculated that the aqueous concentration of glycine in the earth's primeval oceans should have been 10^{-27} moles per liter of water. This value is so small it may be safely described as "infinite dilution." Hull states: "Similar calculations for more complex amino-acids yield smaller concentrations."[23]

Since we are speaking of the decomposition of amino acids as they drift down through the earth's primeval atmosphere, it would be appropriate to speak of their "half-life" of existence. Now, a half-life is simply the length of time required for one-half of an original amount of a given substance to

22. Miller and Urey, p. 245.
23. D. E. Hull, "Thermodynamics and Kinetics of Spontaneous Generation," *Nature*, *186* (1960), p. 693.

decay or decompose. A thirty-day half-life for glycine means that one-half of an original amount of glycine would have decomposed after a period of thirty days. Hull did, in fact, estimate the half-life of glycine to be thirty days, which is much shorter than the half-life required for transport of the molecule from the stratosphere to the earth's surface. He, therefore, concludes: "Thus, 97 percent of the glycine would be decomposed before it could reach the surface." Hull's concluding remarks are particularly relevant to our present discussion:

> The conclusion from these arguments presents the most serious obstacle, if indeed it is not fatal, to the theory of spontaneous generation. First, thermodynamic calculations predict vanishingly small concentrations of even the simplest organic compounds. Secondly, the reactions that are invoked to synthesize such compounds are seen to be much more effective in decomposing them. . . . The physical chemist, guided by the proved principles of chemical thermodynamics and kinetics, cannot offer any encouragement to the biochemist, who needs an ocean full of organic compounds to form even lifeless **coacervates** . . . [emphasis added]. But the fact that a chemist can carry out an organic synthesis in the laboratory does not prove that the same synthesis will occur in the atmosphere or open sea without the chemist.[24]

Hull's calculations and conclusions proved unsettling to the mechanistic materialists. J. D. Bernal reviewed Hull's paper prior to its publication in *Nature* and commented on Hull's conclusions:

> In other words, the original concept of the primitive soup must be rejected only in so far as it applied to oceans or large volumes of water, and interest must be transferred to reactions in more limited zones.[25]

A. L. Lehninger has also acknowledged that the problem of dissolution or decomposition is a serious paradox in the evolutionary approach to the origin of life:

> But here we come to a paradox. The covalent linkages between the building blocks of proteins, nucleic acids, polysaccharides, and lipids are the result of the removal of the elements of water from successive monomeric units. However, peptide

24. Hull, pp. 693, 694.
25. Bernal, reviewing Hull, in *Nature, 186* (1960), p. 694.

bonds, glycosidic bonds, and ester linkages are thermo-dynamically unstable in dilute aqueous systems; that is, they tend to undergo hydrolysis with a large negative standard-free-energy change, so that at equilibrium in dilute aqueous systems only small amounts of such linkages can exist. In order for primordial polypeptides and polynucleotides to have accumulated in the sea, the rate of their formation must have exceeded the rate of their degradation.[26]

Lehninger has precisely pointed out the paradox. In order for present statements of mechanistic materialism to satisfactorily explain the origin of life, the rate of formation of bio-polymers in Stage Two *must* have exceeded their rate of decomposition. The paradoxical experimental fact is that rates of degradation, decay, and dissolution far exceed the expected rate of spontaneous formation of bio-polymers. Typical procedure on the part of the materialist in this area of thought is to recognize the existence of the paradox and then to effectively ignore it. We insist that the paradox cannot simply be ignored; one must deal with it. Again, it is suggested that, although woefully lacking in experimental support, the line of thought among the materialists is the following:

Presupposition: Matter is the only eternal entity.
Observation: Here we are.
Conclusion: Life spontaneously evolved from inorganic matter.

In summary, the following assumptions are made by mechanistic materialism for Stage Two of the origin-of-life hypothesis:

1. Stage One was effective.
2. The right amount of the right kind of energy was available.
3. The rate of decomposition of products did not exceed their rate of formation (this appears to be false).
4. There existed some "ordering principle" within matter alone.

We have absolutely no positive evidence that any of the above assumptions is true. In each case the materialist is making an a priori argument, assuming that matter is the only reality. This is a philosophical statement which has not and cannot be verified.

26. Lehninger, p. 774.

Stage Three: Origin of Primordial Life

It is questionable as to whether any significant experimental work at all has been accomplished at this stage in the origin-of-life problem. There have been two approaches to the hypothetical models for the origin of a

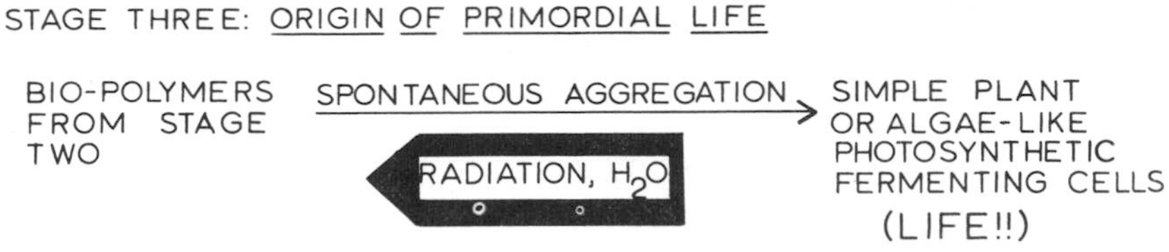

STAGE THREE: ORIGIN OF PRIMORDIAL LIFE

BIO-POLYMERS   SPONTANEOUS AGGREGATION   SIMPLE PLANT
FROM   STAGE   ────────────────────────▶   OR ALGAE-LIKE
TWO   PHOTOSYNTHETIC
                 RADIATION, H_2O FERMENTING CELLS
                                               (LIFE!!)

Fig. 29.   Stage Three of the origin-of-life hypothesis

primordial cell starting from bio-polymers or macromolecules. Both models tend to ignore the rate or time factor involved, inasmuch as decomposition of any form of primeval life would have been greatly enhanced by radiation and dissociation due to hydrolysis in the earth's primeval waters. Indeed, we have no basis for calculating or even estimating the time that would be required for such an event as the spontaneous formation of a living cell to occur. Also, there is a severe lack of a model by which bio-polymers could be sufficiently "ordered" to provide a system that could metabolize and reproduce, regardless of how simple it may have been. Green and Goldberger offer the following opinion as to the utter complexity and uncertainty of this stage in the evolution-of-life problem:

> How, then did the precursor cell arise? The only unequivocal rejoinder to this question is that we do not know. Undoubtedly, selection played a role in the process, although the efficiency was probably not as great as in Darwinian evolution. . . . However, the macromolecule-to-cell transition is a jump of fantastic dimensions, which lies beyond the range of testable hypothesis. In this area, all is conjecture. The available facts do not provide a basis for postulating that cells arose on this planet.[27]

One approach to Stage Three suggests that the original or primordial cells functioned in the absence of nucleic acids and genetic systems. A. I. Oparin of the Soviet Union fathered this concept, suggesting that the

27. D. E. Green and R. F. Goldberger, *Molecular Insights into the Living Process* (New York: Academic Press, 1967), pp. 403, 407.

pre-living thing was a **"coacervate droplet"** of cell dimensions in which bio-organic compounds such as amino acids, sugars, heterocyclic bases, and so forth were entrapped. The interaction of chemicals within the supposedly highly viscous droplets constituted what Oparin called "primal metabolism." lism." Coacervate droplets have been made in the laboratory from substances such as gelatin, gum arabic, and ribonucleic acids. However, they are neither uniform nor stable. Coacervate droplets are, therefore, severely lacking as a sufficient model for the pre-living cell. They are totally lacking as a model for primordial life.

An idea similar to the coacervate droplet concept of Oparin has resulted from the work of S. W. Fox of the University of Miami, who has formed "microsphere droplets" from synthetic **"proteinoids"** made in his laboratory. The microspheres are about 2.0 microns in diameter, contain no lipids, are stable at pH 3-7, exhibit "budding" and apparent "division," and when the hydrogen ion concentration is properly adjusted show a double-layer boundary structure resembling a cell membrane. The microspheres presumably bud and divide by a purely physical mechanism of accretion and accumulation of proteinoids from the surrounding aqueous environment. Concerning the plausibility of the microspheres as a life precursor, A. L. Lehninger states:

> Although such models of primitive cells are very plausible, they could not evolve very far without a genetic system. Moreover, such models require that information must have passed from primitive proteins to primitive nucleic acids until a stable genome could develop, a process which has no present-day counterpart.[28]

Another major objection to Fox's microspheres is that his proteinoids are synthesized under conditions which are inconceivable as representing pre-biotic primeval earth conditions. Fox and his students heat solid amino acids containing high concentrations of **aspartic** and **glutamic acids** to $170°$ C. In the absence of water, peptide bonds are formed and proteinlike compounds with molecular weights of 3,000-11,000 result. These he has termed "proteinoids." These substances show weak biological catalytic activity and resemble proteins in terms of solubility, precipitation, hydrolysis, and infrared spectra.[29] The main objection to Fox's proteinoids is

28. Lehninger, p. 784.
29. S. W. Fox, K. Harada, G. Krampitz, and G. Mueller, "Chemical Origins of Cells," *Chemical and Engineering News*, (22 June 1970), pp. 80-84.

that under primordial earth conditions one would not expect anhydrous conditions to exist nor would one expect to find, even in localized areas, such extremely high concentrations of amino acids. Neither was heat alone a likely primordial energy source, except around volcanoes and hot springs.

The second approach to Stage Three was stated by the geneticist Muller in 1929 and suggests that life first began with the **abiotic** formation of one or more **genes**. In other words, this theory is based on the assumed primacy of nucleic acids. According to this approach a simple virus could have been the pre-living thing, as has been suggested earlier. Most work in this area pertaining to the origin of life is purely speculative at present, but the concept is gaining acceptance as our knowledge of the chemistry of genetics increases. At present it is inconceivable that nucleic acids in a self-reproducing, energy-conserving system independent of numerous proteins, lipids, and carbohydrates could have exhibited the properties of even the simplest form of life.

Semi-Quantitative Probability Considerations

Inasmuch as the materialistic hypothesis assumes that life originated as the result only of the chance interaction of particles of matter in accordance with the laws of nature, it seems that one should be able to apply probability calculations to test the validity of the hypothesis. The fact is that even the simplest forms of life are so utterly complex that this precludes the making of exact probability statements concerning the likelihood of a spontaneous generation of life. However, semi-quantitative probability calculations of this sort invariably question the validity of spontaneous generation and natural selection as adequate explanations for the origin of life and its subsequent evolution. Before proceeding, it would be well to return to chapter 2, where the improbability of spontaneous generation was treated qualitatively, as well as review chapter 3, which emphasized the utter complexity of even the theoretically simplest form of life.

Probability is a very tricky branch of mathematics which deals with the degree of certainty or uncertainty that an event will happen or not happen. *Nothing is ever proved by probability statements;* however, as we will soon see, it becomes essential for us to assume that events of a very low probability *do not* occur but that events with a very high probability are *certain* to occur. An event with a probability of one is an absolute certainty, whereas an event with a probability of zero is an absolute impossibility. A coin has two sides, and if it is "unloaded" or "undoctored" it has a probability of one-half or 0.5 for turning up heads and an equal probability for turning up tails. It should be recognized that actually a heads or tails probability in this case is a little less than one-half or 0.5, because there exists a finite, but very small, probability that the coin will land on edge. However, this is a very small probability, and we assume that it does not occur. The landing on edge is, therefore, assigned a probability of zero and is ignored.

The mechanistic materialist agrees that the spontaneous generation of life is an event with a very low probability; however, he would have us believe that *given indefinite time* any event of low probability will inevitably occur. To a point we would tend to agree. However, the spontaneous generation of life does not involve *one* event of low probability; it involves *a long series of events,* each with a very small probability. The total probability of a series of low-probability events becomes vanishingly smaller and smaller as the length of the series increases. In the case of the spontaneous generation of life, we are dealing with a series of events that is very long, to say the least. Certainly, for all practical purposes the probability of this series of events may safely be regarded as zero. To assume that this long series of improbable events is inevitable violates all reason. It is, furthermore, a direct contradiction of a fundamental law of probability which, according to the eminent French mathematician of probability, Emile Borel, is known as the single law of chance. This law states: Phenomena with very small probabilities *do not occur.*[30]

The single law of chance is fundamental and must be assumed as reliable. For instance, when one boards an airplane or drives off in an automobile, he must assume, for his own sanity if nothing else, that the improbable event of a fatal collision will not occur. Also, one assumes that the low probability event of a flipped coin landing on edge will not occur. However, we are aware that these events of "improbability" do occasionally take place. The probability that either of these events will occur somewhere in the world today to someone is very large; they are, in fact, certain to occur, but one must assume that they will not happen to him. The Christian assumes that the event of a fatal collision will not occur, but

30. E. Borel, *Probabilities and Life,* trans. M. Baudin (New York: Dover Publishing, Inc., 1962), p. 1.

he prepares himself for the event by living a Christian life and taking out appropriate insurance policies so that his family will be somewhat protected in case of disaster.

Now, the above discussion should illustrate the assumption of the single law of chance: Phenomena with very small probabilities *do not occur.* However, the probabilities of the above events are very large in comparison to the likelihood that the long series of improbable events inherent in the spontaneous generation of life will occur. In fact, the events of an automobile collision or a coin landing on edge and the spontaneous generation of life are not comparable at all. The probability of the spontaneous generation of life can perhaps better be compared to the following examples of events of low probability.

The physicist and the mathematician will agree that within any period of time there is a finite probability that one's study desk will rise "spontaneously" from the floor by the space of X inches and then fall with a thud. All that is necessary for this unlikely event to occur is for all gas molecules above and below the desk to move upward simultaneously by the space of X inches and then suddenly resume their random motion. The fact that this is a "probable" event does not necessarily mean that it will inevitably occur, even given indefinite time. The single law of chance insists that we must assume that this event is not inevitable and it *will not occur.* Furthermore, we do not expect the event to occur, even given indefinite time.

Also, we do not expect a room full of monkeys typing in a room full of typewriters to produce a copy of Goethe in its German (or even English) text. Furthermore, we must assume that this event is not only not inevitable, but that it will not happen at all, even given indefinite time.

In addition, we do not expect that life and all its multiplicities would spontaneously arise from terrestrial matter. This is, indeed, widely admitted to involve a series of events, each with a very small probability; and we can best assume that the long series of improbable events will not spontaneously happen at all, even given indefinite time. But we are reminded that we do not have indefinite time; we are limited to finite time: the age of the earth. As pointed out earlier, the real problem in the origin of life is not only a thermodynamic problem, but it is also a kinetic or rate problem.

The problem, of course, is in the fact that we cannot specify exactly what the probability of the spontaneous generation of life is. Could we do this, and could we specify the rate at which nature was taking its "chances," we could predict that within a given period of time life should spontaneously evolve. At best we can talk in terms, for example, of the probability of the formation of a single protein molecule. We can then get some feeling for the probability of the spontaneous generation of life by realizing that even the simplest form of life is perhaps thousands of times more complex than a single protein molecule.

No single probability calculation of the following sort is or can be free of objection. One can always find some critical point to emphasize when speaking of probability statements. We emphasize a point made earlier: *Nothing is ever proved by probability statements.* However, we also emphasize that it is a violation of logic to assume that events of near zero probability *must occur within a finite period of time.* The following calculation is certainly not free of objection and neither can it be completely pushed aside as irrelevant.

The Swiss physicist, Charles Eugene Guye, calculated the probability of the chance formation of a simple protein molecule of molecular weight 20,000 (much too simple to exhibit any "life principle"), a dissymmetrical degree of 0.9 (another simplifying assumption), and consisting of only two elements (compare with 4-10 elements). The probability of the chance formation of a single simple molecule as this, according to Guye, would require (at the rate of 500 trillion "chances" per second) 10^{243} billion years. The latter figure is inconceivably large: it is one followed by 243 zeros. Concerning Guye's calculation, the French science philosopher du Nouy says:

> But we must not forget that the earth has only existed for two billion years and that life appeared about one billion (1×10^9) years ago as soon as the earth had cooled. We thus find ourselves in the case of the player who does not have at his disposal the time necessary to throw his die often enough to have one single chance of obtaining his series. . . .[31]

Concerning the possibility of the initial chance formation of two or three such molecules, Pelletier, head of the department of chemistry at the University of Georgia and internationally recognized natural products chemist, says that this is "equivalent to admitting a miracle."[32]

31. P. LeCompte du Nouy, *Human Destiny* (New York: Longmans, Green, and Co., Inc., 1947), pp. 35-36.
32. S. W. Pelletier, V. A. Coulter Public Lecture, presented at the University of Mississippi, 25 March 1965.

Let us remember that modern laboratory scientists are experimenting in the twentieth century and attempting to interpret what "might have been" billions of years ago. We do not object to their experimentation or even their hypotheses. We do object to their overlooking the philosophical nature of the problem and ignoring the theological alternative, as well as their holding up their hypotheses as factual. They do not know what primitive earth conditions were, and they are extrapolating from highly ordered laboratory test-tube experiments to the open atmosphere and the ruthless terrestrial primitive earth. Even if life is successfully synthesized in all of its complexity in a modern laboratory, the only real thing that has been demonstrated is that intelligence was required as the ordering principle. *If intelligence is required in the twentieth century, it must have been required on the primitive earth.*

As we inquire deeper and deeper into the problem of our origin we are certain to reach a point beyond which no further experimental progress can be made. To inquire beyond this point one must resort to philosophical, metaphysical, or theological considerations. Furthermore, the inquiry demands a leap of faith into a realm that is not testable by experimental science. Every person who seriously considers the question of his origin must, sooner or later, stand at the edge of this philosophical precipice. There are only two ways to leap. One is toward the totally unsubstantiated materialistic presupposition that matter is the only eternal principle. It is hoped that this text has demonstrated that the materialistic presupposition is woefully inadequate, at least as far as the origin of life is concerned. The only logical alternative to mechanistic materialism is the theological alternative. This basically reduces to Biblical revelation and, in particular, a consideration of Genesis 1, which is taken up in the next chapter.

CHAPTER 5

OBSERVATIONS AND
REFLECTIONS ON GENESIS 1

Introduction

It is with a good measure of apprehension that a discussion of Genesis 1 is undertaken. Many volumes have been written on this marvelous chapter of God's Word, and there is obviously no unanimity of opinion as to the explicit meaning of the text within either liberal or conservative areas of thought. I certainly am not so presumptuous as to believe that my comments will settle any debates or "clear the air," so to speak, with respect to any one controversy which has arisen from Genesis 1.

It should not disturb us that we have different views on Genesis 1 as long as we do not deny the trustworthiness of Scripture or hold in question its inspiration. Central to the reformation movement was the concept of the priesthood of all Christian believers, evidenced in Martin Luther's Ninety-five Theses which he nailed to the door of the Castle church in Wittenberg on October 31, 1517. Three years later Luther elaborated on this concept in a tract entitled *An Address to the Christian Nobility of the German Nation,* in which he made clear that every Christian has the responsibility and the right to interpret the Bible for himself because he is a priest in the kingdom of God.[1] The concept of the priesthood of believers is, indeed, Biblical (Heb. 7; Rev. 1:6); and it continued to be a battle cry during the restoration movement. Only in recent years has this principle seemed to lose emphasis in our pulpits. Relative to our present discussion, the Biblical concept of the priesthood of all Christians simply means that you do not need me to tell you what you should believe about Genesis 1, and neither should my understanding of Genesis 1 be dependent on your views. New Testament Christians are not bound by creedal or doctrinal predispositions as are members of some

---

1. F. W. Mattox, *The Eternal Kingdom* (Delight, Ark.: Gospel Light Publishing Co., 1961), p. 246.

religious bodies, nor should they be bound by human tradition. It is, indeed, unfortunate if one would sacrifice personal understanding of any Scripture, including Genesis 1, in order to make his understanding conform to an intangible mold that has been created by human tradition. Perfect freedom should be tolerated in our understanding of the Bible as long as the trustworthiness, integrity, or inspiration of Scripture is not clearly violated or questioned. Even then, correction should be undertaken with patience and Christian love.

Let me now very briefly mention the framework within which the following observations and reflections are made. First, the following discussion is set forth in the humble expectation that, in part, some will disagree with what is stated here. I make no pretense of possessing scholarship in the area of Biblical criticism. Second, this discussion is not offered in a spirit of dogmatism and intolerance toward those who may disagree. Third, I speak first as a Christian and secondarily as a scientist. As such I recognize certain irreconcilable differences between the pronouncements of science concerning origins and the general impressions a person gets from reading Genesis 1. However, I feel that this dissonance need not necessarily be disturbing to a Christian's faith. Fourth, I have absolute confidence in the integrity and trustworthiness of the text of Genesis 1 and I look upon this text as being a sketchy but *factual* account of the creation events. However, I am not so presumptuous as to imply that I know all the creation *facts* implied in the text of Genesis 1. Fifth, I admit to possessing a simple, childlike, and perhaps naive faith in the message of Genesis 1. However, in places I have attempted to reconcile in my own mind some of the apparent disharmony between Genesis 1 and scientific discovery. Doubtless, one of the greatest difficulties that confronts a Christian scientist in his approach to Genesis 1 is the problem of the age of the earth and *when* the creation events took place.

The Age of the Earth

This is no attempt to give either a critique or a summary of the various techniques available for dating the age of the earth. That is certainly beyond the scope of this text. However, an effort will be made to put into perspective Biblical implications and scientific statements bearing on the age of the earth.

I would first remind the reader that it is not within the realm of scientific investigation to discover absolutes. Hence, we do not expect any scientific dating method to give us an exact age for the earth. I know of no dating technique that presumes such accuracy. We should not even be surprised if various dating techniques differ somewhat in their estimated ages for the earth. However, when we discover that two or more different dating techniques are in general agreement as to the age of the earth, then we have good reason to accept the conclusions of the methods. This is particularly true if the methods are employed by different investigators and the conclusions can be repeatedly cross-checked.

From the many scientific dating methods one gets the very strong general impression that the earth is quite ancient. In fact, one does not need to rely on dating techniques to get this impression. For example, we can see with our own eyes the evident slow, methodical manner in which the Colorado River has eroded away stratum after stratum of the earth's crust until the great Grand Canyon has been gouged out, revealing a myriad of stratagraphic layers apparently composed of different materials and deposited at different times prior to the erosion. We are impressed with the vastness of time required for water filtering through limestone to dissolve enough material away to form the Carlsbad Caverns in New Mexico and Mammoth Cave in Kentucky. We also have witnessed water slowly dripping from the ceilings of underground caverns and gradually depositing its minerals, causing great stone icicles or stalactites to be formed as well as their inverted counterparts called stalagmites. Undersea caverns have also been discovered which contain stalactites and stalagmites, strongly suggesting that once these areas were above water level for long periods of time. Limestone quarries, mainly consisting of aquatic shell deposits and often found at very high elevations, cause us to believe that once much of North America was covered by the sea. Petrified wood, oil, and coal deposits apparently of biological origin, the very existence of fossils, sedimentation rates, the apparent drift of the continents, and a number of radioactive isotope dating methods all lead us to the very strong impression that the earth is quite ancient.

Not only does the earth give us an impression of antiquity, but the moon does as well. Young moon craters have "fresh" sharp edges, whereas old craters are ghostly in appearance, possessing rounded-off edges apparently due to vast periods of slow lunar erosion by cosmic dust bombardment.

Table 2 summarizes the various techniques, methods, and resultant ages obtained for the age of the earth. Of the scientific methods indicated for dating the age of the earth, the methods appearing to be the most accurate

TECHNIQUE	METHOD	AGE IN YEARS
Radioactive decay	U^{238}/Pb^{206} ; U^{235}/Pb^{207} Pb^{206}/Pb^{207}	Up to three billion
Radioactive decay	Th^{232}/Pb^{208}	Up to three billion
Radioactive decay	Rb^{87}/Sr^{87}	Up to four billion
Radioactive decay	K^{40}/Ar^{40}	Up to three billion
Radioactive decay*	C^{14}	Does not apply above 45,000 years
Tidal friction	Earth-moon system	2.4 billion
Ocean salinity	Ocean salt accumulation	over 100 million
Sedimentation	Stratum sedimentation rates	350 million
Expansion of universe**	Red shift	Up to 10 billion
Biblical chronology	Ussher and Lightfoot[2]	About 6000

Table 2.   *Age of the earth in years as indicated by*
various dating techniques

* *Since this method does not apply above 45,000 years, it cannot be used
to date the age of the earth.*
** *This method is used to estimate the age of the universe.*

2. B. Ramm, *The Christian View of Science and Scripture* (Grand Rapids: Wm. B.
Eerdmans Publishing Co., 1956), p. 174.

and reproducible are the radioactive techniques. However, these techniques have come under sharp criticisms by certain individuals, especially those who argue for a young earth.

It is, indeed, true that the radioactive methods are based on certain unproved assumptions or presuppositions; but, after all, this is true of every scientific endeavor. It is also true, as can be seen from Table 2, that there is not one hundred percent agreement among the dates obtained from the various radioactive methods. This is true mainly because the range of results obtained reflects the use of different samples which have different ages. In each case, the determined age is dated from the time that the rock solidified from its former molten or semifluid state. The significant fact is that when different investigators, using different techniques, date a given rock sample, they tend to come up with ages that are generally in agreement. This tends to lend credibility to the radioactive method. It is also true that any determined age will have only a certain percentage of accuracy. R. L. Whitelaw claims a "probable error" in the Potassium^{40}-Argon^{40} analysis to be over fifty percent.[3] It is seriously doubtful that the error is this great; but, even if it is, one is still talking in terms of 1.5 billion years for the age of the earth, which is quite ancient. In fact, an error of ninety-nine percent in the method leaves one with an earth that is 30 million years old. To get a value of 6,000 years for the age of the earth one would have to assume an error of 99.9998 percent for *each of the major radioactive methods.* Inasmuch as the different methods employ different techniques and, in some cases, different assumptions, an error of such a magnitude as this is quite incredible.

It is certainly true that during the history of the earth there have occurred many catastrophes such as the Great Flood of Genesis 6, earthquakes, and volcanic eruptions which have wrought radical changes in the earth's surface over relatively short periods of time. It is not necessary to believe that all changes that have occurred on the earth's surface have been brought about by the slow processes that we see working today. I am, therefore, not a strict uniformitarianist. At the same time, however, I see no reason why I should stretch my imagination in order to suppose that a few catastrophic events over a relatively short period of a few thousand

3. R. L. Whitelaw, "Radiocarbon Confirms Biblical Creation (and So Does Potassium-Argon)," *Creation Research Society Quarterly* (September 1968), p. 83.

years could have given the earth its general overall appearance of great antiquity.

The Age of Life on Earth

One can afford to be much more positive in making a statement about the age of inorganic, nonliving matter than he can about life itself. The only reliable technique available to us for dating remains of living organisms is the radioactive carbon-14 method. However, this method is greatly limited because of the relatively short half-life of the carbon-14 isotope. As suggested in Table 2, the carbon-14 technique does not apply—and therefore cannot be used—where objects date older than about 45,000 years.

The principle behind this method is very simple. Any living organism, whether plant or animal, tends to assimilate carbon dioxide from the air. This carbon dioxide is assimilated constantly as long as the organism lives. Most of this carbon dioxide contains nonradioactive carbon-12, but some of it contains radioactive carbon-14. When the organism dies, no more carbon dioxide is assimilated and the carbon-14 which was assimilated while the organism lived begins to decay and disappear. Hence, we say that the carbon-14 "clock" is set at the death of the organism. The length of time required for one-half of the carbon-14 to decay is called the half-life of the radioactive carbon. By measuring the amount of carbon-14 in a sample and knowing how rapidly the carbon-14 decays, one can estimate the length of time that the carbon-14 clock has been running.

The disappearance of the carbon-14 due to decay is analogous to sand running out of an hour glass. After so long, all of the sand runs out of the hour glass and no longer can it be used to estimate the amount of time that has lapsed since the hour glass was set. Likewise, after so much of the carbon-14 has decayed or disappeared from a dead organism, one can no longer use this method to date the age of the organism. This point is reached about 45,000 years after the organism dies. The carbon-14 method is very reliable; that is, it has a small percentage error for dating objects that are 10-15,000 years old. However, beyond 15,000 years the percentage error gets progressively larger and larger until the method becomes virtually worthless for dating objects older than about 45,000 years. To be sure, life has been on earth well over 10,000 years. This has been demonstrated many times by carbon-14 dating.

We are all aware that fossils have been assigned dates much greater than 45,000 years. However, carbon-14 *was not used* to date such objects. Other radioactive methods are used in such instances. Furthermore, in the radioactive dating of fossils, one is never dating organic matter; he is always dating inorganic matter that has crystallized in cell cavities of the dead organism. Hence, one is, in fact, not dating a living organism; he is either dating a geological stratum in which a fossil has formed due to sedimentation, or he is dating inorganic matter that has crystallized in cell cavities due to accretion.

It is true that all of the radioactive methods are based on assumptions and presuppositions which cannot be proved or demonstrated to be exact or true. However, it is also a fact that every scientific endeavor is likewise based on similar presuppositions. One can rest assured that if two or more investigators who are using different radioactive methods give approximately the same date for the age of an object, then the age given is at least fairly reliable. Even in the case of fossils, the determined ages are probably also reliable. However, in this case, there does remain a very substantial question: "Is one actually dating the age of an organism or is he merely dating much older inorganic matter that happened to crystallize in the cell cavities of the dead organism?"

Evidences of God's Design and Purpose in Radioactivity

The radioactive nucleus is a part of God's creation just as is any other aspect of nature. Hence, it is not unexpected that we find evidence of God's design and purpose in radioactivity. Consider carefully the following:

1. Radioactive decay rates are regular, constant, and uniform. We have no reason to believe that decay rates are affected by any factors external to the nucleus of the radioactive atom. Pressure, temperature, or even chemical combination does not alter decay rates. It is this fact of unalterable decay rates that allows one to estimate the age of an object. The fact that *overall* radioactive decay rates are consistent and orderly rather than haphazard and disorderly, evidences God's design in nature, because God is Himself consistent and orderly.

2. The use of the word *overall* in the last sentence leads us to a

second observation that reflects God's purpose and design in radioactivity. One cannot predict exactly when any one radioactive nucleus will decay by the emission of a particle or quantum of radiation. However, one can very accurately predict the *probability* that *some* nucleus within a population of several radioactive atoms will decay within a given period of time. It is this overall prediction that can be determined accurately and is constant with time. However, the un-Christian and atheistic philosophy of materialistic determinism would have us believe that we should be able to predict exactly when any given nucleus will decay. The fact that this cannot be done stands as perhaps nature's greatest blow to materialistic determinism.

3. There is a second means by which the radioactivity of certain elements stands in opposition to the philosophy of materialism. Materialism claims that matter is eternal. However, if this were true, then all radioactive nuclei would have long ago decayed to stable nonradioactive elements. The very fact that the elements are naturally radioactive insists that all radioactive time clocks were set at some moment in time in the past. The Biblical concept of creation satisfies this requirement, whereas the materialistic concept of the eternity of matter does not satisfy this requirement. The fact that radioactive clocks are reset when an ore sample is melted does not minimize the force of this argument.

4. The world is rapidly using up its supply of disposable energy sources, such as natural gas, coal, and oil. However, due to the fact of radioactivity, it appears that the nuclei of atoms, such as uranium, plutonium, and others, offer us a virtually inexhaustible supply of energy. One cannot help but wonder if this is not God's means of making available to mankind a limitless supply of energy if it is used in a peaceful and productive manner.

5. It is ironic that some overzealous Christian antagonists of radioactive dating methods have attacked the carbon-14 method when, in fact, it is precisely by this method that the Dead Sea Scrolls were shown to predate the Christian era. These scrolls have given us substantial evidence that the texts of our Old Testament documents were essentially unaltered during transmission over a period of 2,000 years. Again, we emphasize that the carbon-14 method is essentially accurate in dating objects up to 15,000 years old. Its accuracy continues to diminish until the method becomes unusable at around 45,000 years.

In summary, it is evident that there is the same amazing detail, variety, and design in the infinitesimal atom as there is in the infinitely large universe. The Christian would be remiss and perhaps unappreciative if he did not recognize the design and purpose in the radioactivity of atomic nuclei and give God the praise for it all. Let us learn to use radioactivity as a tool to help us discover more about God's creation rather than to criticize and censure.

Why Do Some Insist on a Young Earth?

But why do some people insist that the earth is relatively recent in origin? First, I feel that it is because one gets the general impression from the Bible that the earth is young. But nowhere in the Bible do we find when or how long ago the creation events of Genesis 1 occurred. It is true that Biblical chronology leaves one with the general impression of a relatively recent origin for man, but even then few are willing to insist that Biblical chronology is sufficiently accurate and complete so as to enable one to accurately date man's origin.[4]

Furthermore, in this present discussion we are not talking about the age of man or even the age of life on earth. We are talking about the age of inorganic, nonliving, terrestrial matter. One point that I wish to make very clear is this: if I must choose between a specific and clearly defined statement of Biblical revelation and a scientific assumption or presupposition, I will most certainly choose Biblical revelation. However, we must be most careful not to read into Scripture information which the Holy Spirit in inspiring the text did not intend for us to get out of the text. There is no explicit and well-defined statement in Biblical revelation as to the age of the earth or to the age of life on the earth. Furthermore, we should resist the temptation to take a general impression which we get from Biblical revelation and crystallize it into an absolute truth that we bind on others. Some religious groups have done this in areas of Biblical revelation, to their great harm and apostasy.

The statements "God created" (Genesis 1 and elsewhere) and "God spoke and it was done; He commanded and it stood fast" (Ps. 33:9) do not

4. J. W. Sears, *Conflict and Harmony in Science and the Bible* (Grand Rapids: Baker Book House, 1969), pp. 17-20.

explicitly rule out some sort of process. Now, if the days of Genesis 1 are taken as twenty-four-hour days, then that certainly rules out any process extending over vast periods of time. The days of Genesis 1 could easily have been twenty-four-hour days and the earth still date to great antiquity, provided that indefinite periods of time separated the six creation days. According to this view, the creation events were *fiat* events: God spoke and the event was accomplished over a very short period of time. Whether or not *process* was involved, one cannot say. Other possible ways of viewing Genesis 1 will be mentioned later.

A second reason that I would suggest why some people insist that the earth is recent in origin is that they believe an ancient-earth concept opens the door for evolution. This position is disturbing for two reasons. First, it is utterly illogical and unscientific. Do we reject the concept of hybridization and thereby refuse to plant hybrid corn because it opens the door for evolution? Of course not. Neither do we reject the concept of mutations because it opens the door for evolution. Natural selection is a process undeniable to the observant individual, but we do not deny natural selection because it opens the door for evolution. I most emphatically deny that natural selection working through mutations is the *modus operandi* for the hypothesis of general biological evolution, but I do not question the fact of mutations or natural selection.

Second, this fear of opening the door for evolution is disturbing to me because it overlooks the fact that the hypothesis of general evolution is an utterly unworkable process as is presently conceived by the mechanistic materialists. As we have suggested in chapters 1 through 4 of this text, the spontaneous generation of life is a most improbable event. In fact, it takes more faith to believe in spontaneous generation than it takes *not* to believe in it. Yet, the materialist postulates that the spontaneous generation of life must have occurred before the process of general biological evolution could have led to speciation. Furthermore, it is widely admitted that there is no positive evidence, fossil or otherwise, which bridges the gaps of ancestral forms of major families of organisms. It seems that some antagonists to evolutionary theory feel that since biological evolution admittedly requires long periods of time, then in order to oppose evolution one must argue for a young earth. *This reasoning is fallacious because it overlooks the impossibility of the spontaneous generation of life.* However, if the spontaneous generation of life is maintained to be impossible, it does not matter if the earth is billions of years old. If life cannot spontaneously arise, it most certainly cannot evolve!

Theistic Evolution

Theistic evolution is sometimes offered as a compromise between the scientific concept of an ancient earth shaped by process and the Biblical demand for God as creator. Theistic evolution takes on about as many different forms as there are individuals professing it. However, it is generally true that in theistic evolution God becomes sort of an "honorary first cause." Evolution is taken in the classical atheistic sense, except that God has been inserted into the scheme. God has, therefore, according to theistic evolution, created the natural laws; and chance processes have taken over from there. As the animal body evolved from a single, primordial cell, God is supposed to have created man's spirit and placed it into the body of a brute beast, at which time man became a living soul.

It is my firm belief that the Christian who accepts general biological evolution in a "theistic" sense is making an unnecessary compromise. The following eight arguments are offered in support of this thesis. However, in spite of these objections it is realized that the creationist has much more in common with the theistic evolutionist than he has with atheistic mechanistic determinism.

1. Even if God is inserted into the concept of evolution and spontaneous generation, the basic idea is still the same. Putting God in does not make evolution any more sound scientifically and, if anything, it makes evolution less scientific. General evolution still remains a hypothesis based on several other hypotheses, none of which is capable of experimental verification. The concept of evolution and spontaneous generation of life is still a faith in a series of historical events; *it is not a verified scientific fact.*

2. God merely becomes the creator of natural law, and we have seen that natural law and probability alone cannot logically account for the origin of life. The spontaneous generation of life still remains as the end product of a long series of highly improbable events.

3. There still remains a lack of evidence for the earliest forms of pre-Cambrian life, as predicted by the evolutionary hypothesis. Likewise, there are no transition fossils linking major ancestral forms of life.

4. Whether or not God is inserted into the concept, it is still unscientific to draw unwarranted conclusions from observations in science. This is precisely what evolutionists have done. To this end, the following statement by Julian Huxley, prince of modern evolutionary thought, is interesting:

> It is possible that I may have been oversweeping in some of my conclusions: and I shall probably be attacked for going beyond the boundaries of science. But I am sure that I have been right in formulating general conclusions of this sort.[5]

5. Evolution is still lacking in a necessary mechanism, unless one thinks of God interceding in and effecting each mutation and operating only through the process of natural selection. If this were true, then God is very inefficient in that it is estimated that the vast majority of mutations are injurious, not resulting in progressive development.[6,7]

6. The Christian theistic evolutionist is basically inconsistent. On the one hand he embraces the miracles of the Lord but on the other he denies the miracle of creation. He believes that God has effected a great miracle at one cosmic event in history—the resurrection of Jesus Christ—but denies that God has effected a miracle at another cosmic event in history—creation.

7. Theistic evolution requires a faith greater than a faith that merely assumes that God is creative but does not question His mode of creation. It is certainly not wrong to be interested in *how* God created life, but it is making an unnecessary compromise for the Christian to assume that God's mechanism for creating man was evolution.

8. Evolution as usually taught in the textbooks remains atheistic, regardless of whether or not the Christian believes that God had a part

5. J. Huxley, *Evolution in Action* (New York: Harper and Row, Publishers, Inc., 1953), p. viii.
6. C. P. Martin, "A Non-Geneticist Looks at Evolution," *American Scientist, 41:1* (January 1953), p. 100.
7. J. F. Crow, "Ionizing Radiation and Evolution," *Scientific American, 201:3* (September 1959), pp. 138-160.

in it. No recognized proponent of the hypothesis maintains that evolution is the medium through which a force outside of nature has created man.

The very nature of the problem forbids one from ever knowing *factually* that general biological evolution has occurred, either with or without God. The evolutionary hypothesis is a philosophically based faith and should not be accepted as fact at the expense of another faith or hypothesis that attempts to account for the origin of life. Theistic evolution is an unnecessary compromise for the Christian. The first verse of the Bible is a presupposition which one should be perfectly willing to accept both as a scientist and as a Christian.

The simplicity and profundity of the creation statements of Genesis 1 are a tribute to the inspiration of Scripture. What God *did not* tell us about the creation events is perhaps as significant as what He *did* tell us. Had God described His mode of creation in terms that would have been understood by the people contemporary with Moses or Abraham, the Bible would most certainly have become obsolete and would have been discarded long ago as unscientific and untrue. Had creation been described mechanistically in Genesis exactly as God caused it to happen, then the Book of Genesis would most likely not have been accepted by its first readers because such an explanation would not have been comprehended at that time and probably could not be comprehended by us today. God has surmounted this problem by simply leaving out any reference to His particular mode of operation in creation. It seems to me that one can best look at Genesis 1 with a childlike faith and accept it as a simple, beautiful, profound, and factual statement of creation. I would, however, be suspect of anyone who professes to know all the facts of the creation events implied in Genesis 1.

The New Testament on Genesis 1

Perhaps the best commentary on Genesis 1 is the New Testament. It is, therefore, notable that the New Testament writers looked on Genesis 1 as a factual and historical account of creation events. Christ taught that at the beginning of creation God made man and woman (Mark 10:6). John identified Jesus Christ as the preexistent Word of God, without whom nothing was made that was made (John 1:1, 3, 14). The apostle Paul reaffirmed the creative activity of God in and through Jesus Christ (Rom. 1:19, 20; Col. 1:16), by whom Christians are also through faith to understand that the universe was framed (Heb. 1:3; 11:3). Perhaps there is no clearer statement of the divine *fiat* in creation than Paul's statement in II Corinthians 4:6: "For God, who commanded the light to shine out of darkness. . . ." In his Athenian sermon Paul exclaimed that God made the world and all things in it (Acts 17:24), and Peter alluded to creation by the Word of God and the earth emerging out of water (II Peter 3:5). It is notable that the New Testament writers make no reference to *process* in creation, for or against. They seem to simply accept at face value the fact of the divine fiat in creation, supposing that the creation of all things was through Jesus Christ, the Word, and that God's creation was good.

Different Concepts of Genesis 1

Numerous concepts of Genesis 1 are extant. It is beyond the scope of this present effort to summarize and describe these concepts. Nevertheless, the essential features of the more prominent concepts, including the length of time demanded by each and objections to the concepts, are given in Table 3. For a more detailed discussion of several of these concepts, one may see the discussion by Bernard Ramm.[8]

A Preferred Approach to Genesis 1

From scholarly considerations there has arisen a multiplicity of concepts of Genesis 1, as is evident in Table 3. For example, two widely different concepts develop, depending on whether one regards verse 1 as a dependent clause or an independent clause. Additional alternatives arise depending on whether the Hebrew *yom* implies a twenty-four-hour day or an indefinite period of time. Still other views arise if one assumes a time gap between verse 1 and verse 2, or if one assumes time gaps between the six individual days of Genesis 1. It is, furthermore, very frustrating to find that Biblical scholarship has literally picked to pieces individual words of Genesis 1 in an apparent effort to find hidden meanings. This reading between the lines is regrettable; for it is not reasonable that the Holy Spirit of God, who inspired this text, intended for a person to read the text so

8. Ramm, pp. 173-229.

critically and legalistically. It is, of course, impossible to completely avoid a critical reading of the text; but one should avoid looking for hidden meanings, overworking individual words, reading between the lines, and especially reading into the text preconceived ideas or notions. In short, Biblical scholarship and criticism have tended to confuse the message of Genesis 1 rather than to clarify it.

It is recommended that the reader approach Genesis 1 with a simple, childlike faith. Basic rules of interpretation should be: (1) do not let your own prejudices or notions alter the meaning of the message; (2) do not look for hidden meanings, resisting any temptation to read between the lines; (3) do not overwork individual words; and (4) do not question the authority, integrity, or trustworthiness of the text. If one does this, it is felt that three basic, uncompromising truths will stand out from Genesis 1. Other matters as to detail may be debatable, but these three truths cannot be compromised. These truths are:

1. God created. That is, all of creation, living and nonliving, was the result of the divine command.
2. God's creation was orderly and progressive, and God pronounced His creation as *good.*
3. Man was created in the image of God and thereby is unique among God's creation.

It seems that in view of the fact that every Christian has both the right and the responsibility to understand the Bible for himself, any concept of Genesis 1 must be tolerated as long as one adheres to the above uncompromising truths from Genesis 1. For this reason, no one particular position on Genesis 1 is taken in this text. A summary of objections to the various concepts of Genesis 1 is given in Table 3. An attitude of tolerance is taken toward several of these concepts.

Observations and Reflections on Genesis 1

The translation of Genesis 1 used below was taken from a text by G. R. Berry.[9] For his translation Berry used the Hebrew text of Baer and

---

9. From the *Interlinear Literal Translation of the Hebrew Old Testament* by G. R. Berry. Copyright © 1946 by Wilcox and Follett Publishing Company, division of Follett Corporation.

CONCEPT	PRINCIPLE
The so-called Literal View	Six 24-hour consecutive days of creation, 4000 B.C. Assumes Bible chronology is complete.
Apparent Age	Same as Literal View but earth has a "built in" age.
Flood Catastrophe	Same as Literal View. Noachian Flood caused all present geological phenomena.
Successive Catastrophe	Same as Literal View. Several catastrophes, including the Great Flood, caused present geological phenomena.
Gap or Restitution	Genesis 1:2; **was=became.** Creation—destruction—restitution. Modern "fossil men" belonged to a pre-Adamic race.
Multiple Gap	Sometimes confused with Day—Age. Six 24-hour creation days separated by indefinite periods. Fiat creation of animal and plant families.
Day—Age	Days of Genesis 1 = geologic ages. **Yom** is used metaphorically. Divine creation activity gradual over long periods.
Revelatory Day	Indefinite time allowed. God revealed the story of creation to Moses in six days.
Theistic Evolution	God created matter and natural law. Life evolved according to current evolutionary thought.
Atheistic Evolution	Everything is a "great coincidence"—matter, life—ALL.

Table 3. A summary of popular Gen-

TIME INVOLVED	OBJECTION
6,000 yrs.	Earth appears older than 6,000 yrs. Overworks Biblical chronology.
6-10,000 yrs. but earth looks much older.	This view implies that God has misled or deceived man. Why fossils? Ancient earth.
6-10,000 yrs.	Ancient earth; radioactive dating. This view attributes too much to the Great Flood of Genesis 6.
6-10,000 yrs.	Ancient earth; radioactive dating. Overworks catastrophism.
Any time for first creation. Re-creation about 6,000 yrs. ago.	Overworks limited parts of Scripture, by putting too much emphasis on one word. However, a favorite view of many fundamentalists.
Any time	No Scriptural basis for assuming indefinite periods between 24-hour days.
Any time	**Day** in Genesis 1 seems to be a 24-hour day. Genesis 1 "reads like" a historical account.
Any time	Genesis 1 reads like history. No Scriptural basis for the principle.
Any time	Requires spontaneous generation of life. Evolution is deficient. Genesis 1 must be understood figuratively.
Any time	Rejects the idea of God. Offers no first cause. Evolution is deficient.

esis 1 concepts and objections to them

Delitzsch, which—in the opinion of many—is the best Masoretic text that has been published. The brackets [ ] have been used by Berry to enclose words *added* in the English which *are* *not* in the Hebrew, and the parentheses ( ) have been used for words which *are* in the Hebrew but of which the English usage requires the *omission*. A word in the Hebrew which has no equivalent in English has been left untranslated by Berry. The Hebrew text reads from right to left; however, for the reader's convenience, the reproduction of the literal translation has been turned around so that it will read from left to right. The word order has been retained just as given by Berry. Limited comments on the literal translation have been made. An effort has been made to simply let the text speak for itself, as well as to avoid reading into the text preconceived ideas or notions.

Literal Translation of Verses 1-5

1 *In the beginning [when] created God the heavens and the earth,*
2 *(and) the earth being a desolation and waste, and darkness [being] upon the face of [the] abyss, and the spirit of God hovering upon the face of*
3 *the waters; then said God: Let light be and light was.*
4 *And saw God the light that [it was] good, and divided God*
5 *between the light and (between) the darkness. And called God to the light day, and to the darkness he called night; and*
    evening was and morning was, day one.

Comments

Verse 1 seems to be a simple yet very profound statement of ultimate or *ex nihilo* (out of nothing) creation. God is the eternally existing first cause of the universe. It is presumptuous to suppose that a vast time interval existed between verses 1 and 2; yet this is a distinct possibility which cannot be excluded. Time is a nonentity with God (II Peter 3:8). The use of "evening" and "morning" implies solarlike days as we know them today, yet mention of the sun is not made until day four. It is, therefore, difficult to imagine how days one through three were literal twenty-four-hour solar days unless the creation of the sun was included in the "heavens" of verse 1 but was not "revealed" or made evident until day four. *Yom* (day) is clearly used to imply indefinite time in Genesis 2:4. Concerning the various ways for translating *yom*, R. F. Surburg of the theology department at Concordia College states:

> In evaluating these various interpretations bear in mind that *yom* occurs no fewer than 1,480 times in the Old Testament and that it is properly translated by over 50 different words, including "time," "life," "today," "age," "forever," "continually" and "perpetually."[10]

Literal Translation of Verses 6-8

6 *And said God: Let be an expanse in the midst of the waters,*

7 *and let it be dividing between waters to waters. And made God the expanse, and he divided between the waters which [were] (from) under*

 (to) the expanse and (between) the waters which [were] (from) above

8 *(to) the expanse; and it was so. And called God (to) the expanse heavens; and evening was and morning was, a day second.*

Comments

The word translated "expanse" here is translated "firmament" in the King James Version and the Revised Standard Version, whereas in the New English Bible the word is rendered "vault." The word is understood here to simply imply "space." It therefore appears that after day two there existed an earth completely covered with water, above which was an expanse and above the expanse additional waters. By some unspecified means light and darkness continued to mark off evening and morning.

Literal Translation of Verses 9-13

9 *And said God: Let be collected the waters (from) under the heavens unto place one, and let be seen the dry land;*

10. From *Darwin, Evolution, and Creation,* edited by Paul A. Zimmerman, copyright 1959 by Concordia Publishing House. Used by permission.

10 *and it was so. And called God to the dry land earth, and to*
   the collection of the waters he called seas; and saw
11 *God that [it was] good. And said God: Let cause to spring*
   forth the earth grass, herb seeding seed, [and] tree of fruit
   making fruit
   after its kind, [in] which [is] its seed (in it), upon the
   earth; and it was so.
12 *And caused to go forth the earth grass, herb seeding seed*
   after its kind, and tree making fruit [in] which [is] its seed
   (in it)
13 *after its kind; and saw God that [it was] good. And evening*
   was and morning was, a day third.

Comments

In general, the world view as implied by the creation events of day two is not altered by the creation events of day three, except that dry land appeared and God caused grass, herbs, and fruit-bearing trees to appear on the land mass. The expressions "Let be seen the dry land" and "Let cause to spring forth the earth grass" do not rule out some sort of process; in fact, to me they subtly imply some sort of process. However, any process could not have involved a vast period of time if day three was a twenty-four-hour day, which again is implied by use of the expressions "evening" and "morning." However, the sun, which is seemingly required to mark off such solar days, has not yet been mentioned. One cannot rule out the possibility of a long time interval between day two and day three. Also, between day three and day four a vast time interval may have existed, during which time differentiation and variation of the plant forms created in day two could have occurred. However, there is no Biblical basis for assuming the existence of these time intervals.

Literal Translation of Verses 14-19

14 *And said God: Let be luminaries*
   in the expanse of the heavens, to divide between the day
   and (between)
   the night; and let them be for signs, and for seasons, and for
   days
15 *and years; and let them be for luminaries in the expanse of*
   the heavens,

*16 to give light upon the earth; and it was so. And made God
    the two
luminaries great; the luminary greater ruling for the day and
    the luminary smaller for ruling the night;
17 and the stars. And put them God
18 in the expanse of the heaven to give light upon the earth,
    and to rule
    in the day and in the night and to divide between the light
    and (between) the darkness; and saw God that [it was]
    good.
19 And evening was and morning was, a day fourth.*

Comments

An interesting expression is found in verse 14: "Let be luminaries *in the expanse* of the heavens." It would appear that the "expanse" of day four is the same as the "expanse," "firmament," "vault," or "space" which was created on day two. However, if one insists on this strictly literal and critical approach to verses 6-8 and 14, he is led to the unusual cosmology for Genesis 1 shown in Figure 30. This world view leaves one feeling a little uneasy, because it is not the world view which modern man has of the universe. This difficulty is very simply avoided if one follows the suggestion made earlier that we not insist upon a strict and critical interpretation of the text but rather approach Genesis 1 with a childlike and unpresumptuous faith.

Four quotations follow from Old Testament commentaries. The first two represent a scholarly and critical approach to the use of the word "firmament," "vault," or "expanse"; whereas the last two take the approach that is recommended here.

Adam Clarke says of the word "expanse" or "firmament" in Genesis 1:6-8: "The word appears to have been used by Moses in a more extensive sense, and to include the whole of the planetary vortex, or the space which is occupied by the whole *solar system*."[11] If Clarke is correct in this statement, then one is left with the uncomfortable conclusion that there were waters above or beyond the solar system, as implied in verse 7 by use of the expression "waters which [were] above the expanse."

---

11. A. Clarke, *Clarke's Commentary, Volume I* (New York: Abingdon Press, n.d.), p. 33.

H. C. Leupold seems to agree that the "firmament" or "expanse" of verse 14 (day four) is, indeed, the same as the "firmament" or "expanse" of verse 6 (day two). Leupold's comment is: "The adverbial modifier 'in the firmament of the heavens' shows the relation of the fourth day's work

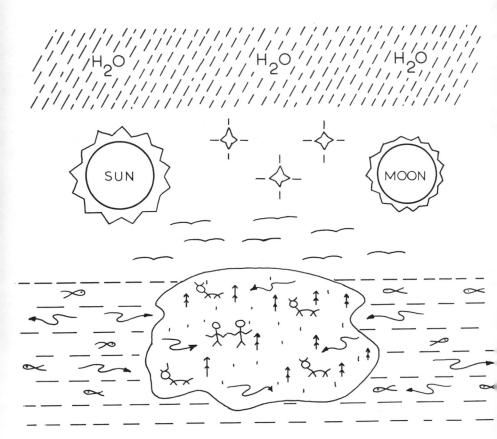

Fig. 30.   A possible Genesis 1 world view

to that of the second."[12] If this statement is strictly true, then it follows that the luminaries which were placed in the firmament of verse 14 were placed in the same firmament (expanse) of verse 6 which separated waters below the firmament from waters above the firmament. This leads to the world view shown in Figure 30.

W. R. Churton, writing in a commentary published in 1889, offered the following attractive and sensible explanation of the apparent world view of Genesis 1: "The heavenly bodies, though really situated in the immense space of heaven, some nearer to the earth and some more remote, are in appearance set in the 'firmament,' through which their light is conveyed to us."[13] This explanation is less critical than the two previously stated and allows that the luminaries of verse 14 were actually placed beyond the

12. H. C. Leupold, *Barnes' Notes: Exposition of Genesis, Vol. I* (Grand Rapids: Baker Book House, 1950), p. 72.
13. W. R. Churton, *Commentary on the Old Testament, Vol. I* (London: 1889), comment on Genesis 1:14.

CODE:

↑ ↑   TREES

,ı١ı;ı ı;ı   GRASS

⌒⌒⌒⌒   FOWL OF AIR, BIRDS

∽∝ ∝   SEA MONSTERS, WHALES, FISHES

⌒⌢⌒   CREEPING THINGS OF THE SEA OR LAND

⤳ ⤳   CATTLE, BEAST OF EARTH, GROUND CREEPERS

♀ᚢ   MAN

"upper waters," but *in appearance* they seemed to be in the firmament or expanse which we know as the atmosphere. Actually, even to modern man, the sun, moon, and stars appear to be in the upper reaches of the earth's atmosphere; and it was only through careful observation that this was shown not to be the case.

A similar solution to the problem has been suggested by the authors of the *Seventh-day Adventist Bible Commentary:* "The expression that they (luminaries) are set in the firmament, or expanse of heaven, is chosen because it is there that the earthly inhabitant sees them."[14]

After giving lengthy consideration to the problem of a world view in Genesis 1, I have come to the conclusion that *there is no world view presented in Genesis 1.* I believe that the intent of Genesis 1 is far too sublime and spiritual for one to presume that it teaches anything at all about a cosmological world view. We do this profound text a great injustice by insisting that there is inherent within the text an argument for any particular world view. However, if one does insist upon a world view as implied by Genesis 1, it would seem that the one suggested in Figure 30 is correct.

Some who assume that the world view shown in Figure 30 is correct for Genesis 1 point out that it is unscientific and in error. Many who take this approach assume that Genesis 1 is, therefore, a nonhistorical, nonfactual account of creation. The world view of Genesis 1 is seen as having been borrowed from the Babylonians or Sumerians. The composition of the Babylonian epic *Enûma elish* ("When above") is dated at perhaps sometime during the First Babylonian Dynasty (1894-1595 B.C.);[15] whereas Moses, who presumably received the creation story of Genesis 1 by inspiration, would have composed the Biblical account sometime after the Exodus, which is thought to have occurred near 1450 B.C.[16] Other pagan accounts of creation legends are also known to be older than the date of the composition of Genesis 1. However, as Figure 31 clearly shows, the pagan accounts could very easily have arisen from the Genesis account during the period that the Genesis account was known only by oral transmission. Just because the dates of composition of *Enûma elish* and

14. *The Seventh-day Adventist Bible Commentary, Vol. I* (Washington, D.C.: Review and Herald Publishing Assn., 1953), p. 212.
15. A. Heidel, *The Babylonian Genesis*, 2nd ed. (Chicago: University of Chicago Press, 1951), p. 14.
16. S. J. Schultz, *The Old Testament Speaks* (New York: Harper and Row, 1960), p. 48.

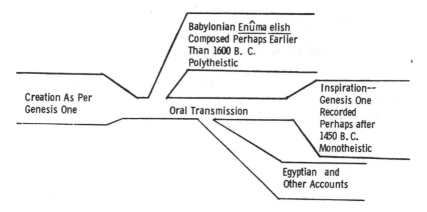

Fig. 31.   Possible derivations of pagan creation accounts from the Genesis account

other pagan creation stories are older than the Genesis account and bear resemblances to it *does not necessarily mean that the Genesis account was based on the pagan accounts.* The very opposite could easily have been the case.

For comparison purposes the first nine verses of Tablet I of the Babylonian *Enûma elish* and the first five verses of Genesis 1 (Revised Standard Version) are reproduced below. A point that bears emphasis is that the dissimilarities of the two accounts are perhaps more significant than their similarities. However, this is not the position that is generally taken by scholarship. The Babylonian account is clearly polytheistic, whereas the Genesis account is monotheistic. In the Babylonian account the spirit of the gods and cosmic matter are coexistent and coeternal, whereas, according to Genesis, God created cosmic matter and, prior to its creation, God existed independent of matter. As one proceeds into the *Enûma elish* he finds it to be crude and grotesque beyond description. A bloody war developed among the gods of the Babylonian legend; and Marduk, the "wisest of the gods," split the skull of the goddess Tiamat, cut her arteries, caused the north wind to carry her blood southward to out-of-the-way places, and finally divided her body into two parts with which he created the universe. Compare this with the simple and profound Biblical statement, "In the beginning God created the heavens and the earth." Additional comparisons and contrasts of the Babylonian epic and the Genesis account are given in Table 4.

	Enûma elish[17]		Genesis 1
1	When above the heaven had not (yet) been named,	1	In the beginning God created the heavens and the earth.
2	(And) below the earth had not (yet) been called by a name;	2	The earth was without form and void, and darkness was upon the face of the deep; and the Spirit of God was moving over the face of the waters.
3	(When) Apsu primeval, their begetter,		
4	Mummu, (and) Tiamat, she who gave birth to them all,	3	And God said, "Let there be light"; and there was light.
5	(Still) mingled their waters together,	4	And God saw that the light was good; and God separated the light from the darkness.
6	And no pasture land had been formed (and) not (even) a reed marsh was to be seen;	5	God called the light Day, and the darkness he called Night. And there was evening and there was morning, one day.
7	When none of the (other) gods had been brought into being,		
8	(When) they had not (yet) been called by (their) name (s, and their) destinies had not (yet) been fixed,		
9	(At that time) were the gods created within them.		

For further comparisons of Genesis 1 and the Babylonian account, readers are encouraged to read the *Enûma elish* for themselves, rather than to depend on comparisons made here or by scholarship.

Literal Translation of Verses 20-23

20 And said God: Let swarm the waters [with] swarms, soul of life, and fowl let fly upon the earth, upon the face of the expanse of the heavens,

21 And created God the sea-monsters great, and all the souls of life that creep, [with] which swarmed the waters, after their kinds, and every fowl of wing after its kind; and saw God

17. A. Heidel, p. 18.

22 *that [it was] good. And blessed them God, saying: Be*
fruitful, and multiply, and fill the waters in the seas,
23 *and the fowl let multiply in the earth. And evening was and*
morning was, a day fifth.

Enûma elish	Genesis 1
Polytheistic	Monotheistic
Grossly materialistic	Spiritual
Gods are humanlike	God is transcendent
Spirit and matter coeternal	Spirit only is eternal
War among the gods	Harmony in heaven
Watery chaos	Watery chaos
Universe created by Marduk dismembering body of goddess Tiamat	"In the beginning God created the heavens and the earth"
Light assumed but existed before luminaries	Light created
Man created last	Man created last
Man created by Ea from blood of a mangled god, Kingu	Man created by God from dust of the earth
Man, servant of the gods	Man, lord of the earth, created in the image of God

Table 4.   Comparison and contrast of Enûma elish *and*
        Genesis 1

Comments

The expressions "Let swarm the waters," "Let fowl fly," "created God the sea monsters great," again do not rule out some sort of process which God could have caused to occur over a short period of time, had this been His will. The word "kind" here is not to be necessarily identified with the word "species" of modern biology. There is the distinct possibility that the Genesis "kind" is not to be compared with any of modern biology's taxonomic classification of plants or animals. To identify "kind" as "species," "order," "family," or even "phyla" is perhaps reading something into the text which should be avoided. We can best acknowledge that we do not know the scientific implication of "kind" in Genesis 1.

The wording "Let fowl fly upon the face of the expanse" is interesting, though I would not press it for precise meaning. It reminds me that recently my little three-year-old daughter, on seeing a jet plane leave a contrail in the sky, remarked to her mother and me, "It scratched the sky, didn't it?" Is it possible, therefore, as has been suggested earlier, that Genesis 1 is a *factual but sketchy* account of what did happen during the creation "week"; but that it was intended for those with a childlike faith, rather than for scientific or Biblical critical scholarship?

Literal Translation of Verses 24-31

24 *And said God, let cause to go forth the earth soul of life*
after its kind, cattle, and creeper, and beast of [the] earth
after its kind,

25 *and it was so. And made God the beast of the earth after its*
kind, and the cattle after its kind, and every creeper of the
ground

26 *after its kind, and saw God that [it was] good. And said*
God: Let us make man in our image, after our likeness; and
let them have dominion over the fish of the sea, and over
the fowl of
the heavens, and over the cattle, and over all the earth, and
over every creeper

27 *that creeps upon the earth. And created God (the) man in*
his image, in the image of God he created him, male

*28 and female he created them. And blessed them God, and
said to them God: Be fruitful, and multiply, and fill the
earth, and subdue it; and have dominion over the fish of
the sea, and over the fowl of the heavens, and over every
beast that creeps*

*29 upon the earth. And said God: Behold, I have given to you
every herb seeding seed which [is] upon the face of all the
earth, and
every tree in which [is] the fruit of tree seeding seed, to
you it shall be*

*30 for food; and to every beast of the earth, and to all the fowl
of the heavens,
and to every creeper upon the earth, in which [is] a soul of
life, [I have given] every greenness of herb for food; and it
was so.*

*31 And saw God all which he had made, and behold, [it was]
good exceedingly; and evening was and morning was, a day
sixth.*

Comments

With verses 24-31 the account of God's creative activities is culminated. Again, it is suggested that some sort of *process* is not strictly excluded and that the "kinds" mentioned here are not necessarily to be identified with the current biological concept of "species." The creation of man is clearly stated to be a divine activity, as well as the creation of woman. Chapter 2 of Genesis recounts the manner (process, if you will) of the creation of woman. The creation of man, and especially woman, cannot logically be construed to have been by any sort of evolutionary process. Mankind is unique among all of God's creation in that man was created in the image of God. This is taken to mean the spiritual image of God rather than a bodily image, inasmuch as man was created flesh and bones. Elsewhere in Biblical revelation we learn that God is spirit, and spirits do not have flesh and bones (John 4:24; Luke 24:39). Finally, it is observed that God found His creation *good.*

SUMMARY

The following points summarize the conclusions which we feel can be safely drawn from a consideration of this study:

1. Mechanistic materialism is inadequate as a philosophical explanation for the ultimate origin of matter and energy.

2. The theological view, which is admittedly a view of faith, is a logical alternative to mechanistic materialism. This is especially true inasmuch as it is seen that the mechanistic material view is also predicated on faith.

3. Mechanistic explanations are not contrary to Christian thought. Only when mechanism is allied with the philosophy of materialism does mechanism conflict with Christianity. This is true because materialism maintains that there is no reality beyond the material realm; that is, there is no spirit.

4. The smallest free-living things known to modern man are so complex as to virtually eliminate their having been formed by chance and random molecular collisions alone, even allowing for great periods of time.

5. We do not know for certain what the condition of the primitive earth was, nor do we know the composition of the primitive earth atmosphere. Present methods for deducing these conditions seem experimentally reasonable; however, the nature of the problem is such that any deductions must be regarded as tentative. Any conclusions drawn from the deductions must, therefore, also be tentative. The mechanistic materialists should not hold up their deductions and conclusions as factual.

6. Scientists who work on the origin-of-life problem are limited to simulating what they suppose were primordial earth conditions some two to four billion years ago. The results of their experiments only reflect what *might have been true* on the primitive earth. All deductions drawn from experimental observations must be regarded as relative and tentative. True objectivity in science is an illusion. A scientist could not recognize an absolute truth of man's origin if he discovered it, because the scientist is limited to working with that which can be measured; and absolutes cannot be measured.

7. The mechanistic material approach to the origin of life is inadequate in terms of offering an explanation for the spontaneous ordering

of simple bio-organic compounds to produce bio-polymers such as proteins and nucleotides. In particular, the materialistic approach is inadequate to explain the spontaneous aggregation of bio-polymers into the pre-living "cell." On the other hand, the theological alternative offers a satisfactory explanation of an "ordering intelligence" which, in a creative moment, brought matter together in such a manner that it became living. The origin of life, therefore, is maintained to be an event that transcends the laws of chemistry and physics. Once created, though, life is maintained by the laws of chemistry, physics, and biology. God and His Word maintain these laws.

8. Genesis 1 is a sketchy but factual account of the creation of both nonliving and living things. God's creative activity was orderly and progressive, and God pronounced His creation as good. Man is unique among God's creation, having been created in the spiritual image of God.

Conclusion:

**Existence of life on earth is an enigma without
the supposition of the existence of God.**

GLOSSARY

Abiogenesis: The **Spontaneous Generation of Life** from inorganic terrestrial matter.

Adenine: See **Heterocyclic Base.**

Aerobic: Aerobic processes occur in the presence of molecular oxygen.

Alanine: See **Amino Acid.**

Algae: A **Chlorophyll**-containing subdivision of a botanical group thought to contain most of the primitive plants.

Amino Acids: Amphoteric (contains both acidic, -COOH, and basic, -NH$_2$, groups) organic compounds containing carbon, hydrogen, nitrogen, oxygen, and sometimes sulfur; an essential chemical "building block" for the synthesis of an essential life substance called **Protein.** Amino acids are ionic in solution, having the general structural formula shown below:

$$\begin{array}{ccc} \text{H} & & \text{O} \\ | & & | \\ \text{H-N}^{+}\text{-} & \text{C} - \text{H-C-O}^{-} \\ | & | & \\ \text{H} & \text{R} & \end{array}$$

The twenty fundamental amino acids are: alanine, valine, leucine, isoleucine, proline, phenylalanine, tryptophan, methionine, glycine, serine, threonine, cysteine, tyrosine, asparagine, glutamine, aspartic acid, glutamic acid, lysine, arginine, and histidine.

Anaerobic: Anaerobic processes occur in the absence of molecular oxygen.

Aspartic Acid: See **Amino Acid.**

Bio-organic: Organic molecules which have important biological function. Bio-organic molecules, such as **Amino Acids** and **Nucleotides,** are molecular precursors of life.

Biogenesis: Life evolving or arising from life, as distinguished from **Abiogenesis,** which means life arising from nonliving matter.

133

Catalyst: A chemical, either organic or inorganic, which speeds up the rate at which a chemical reaction takes place. The catalyst enters into the reaction but emerges unchanged. Hence a small amount of catalyst may promote the formation of many molecules of product. Catalysts are often deactivated by "poisoning" agents.

Cell Membrane: A lipid (fat) membrane about 100 angstroms thick through which things must pass in order to get either into the cell or out of the cell.

Chlorophyll: A complex organic molecule containing a magnesium ion in the center of a **Porphyrin** nucleus. The molecule is essential to the process of **Photosynthesis** and functions by "trapping" light energy and passing it on to other pigment molecules.

Coacervate Droplet: A highly viscous phase, containing a mixture of **Colloidal** particles, which divides into quasiliquid drops. Theoretically, the coacervate drop was a heterogeneous aggregate which contained "life stuff" and was a pre-living cell.

Colloid: Particles usually falling within the size range of 10 angstroms (0.000,000,1 cm.) to 1 micron (0.000,1 cm.). They may be homogeneous or heterogeneous aggregates.

Cytoplasm: Cellular sap consisting of inorganic ions, water, soluble organic and bio-organic chemicals.

Cytosine: See **Heterocyclic Base.**

Denature: To denature a **Protein** or **Polynucleotide** is to cause it to lose the structure or configuration which it tends to possess in its most stable state.

Deoxyribonucleic Acid: (DNA) A polynucleotide containing the **Heterocyclic Bases: Adenine, Thymine, Guanine,** and **Cytosine;** the sugar **Deoxyribose;** and phosphate residues. DNA usually occurs as double-stranded molecules wound around one another in a double helix. The molecular weight may range from a few million to 100 million. This corresponds to several thousand **Nucleotide** monomer units. DNA carries hereditary information in a coded form as well as other information which ultimately determines the biochemical make-up of the living cell.

Deoxyribose: A five-carbon atom sugar molecule that is identical to **Ribose** except that the former has a methylene group ($-CH_2-$) at position number two instead of a hydroxyl group ($-OH$). **Deoxyribose** is essential to the formation of the **Polynucleotide Deoxyribonucleic Acid (DNA).** See **Ribose.**

Endoplasmic Reticulum: A continuous opening from the outer membrane to the nuclear membrane of a cell.

Enzyme: An organic molecule, a **Protein**, which catalyzes biochemical reactions. Enzymes are much more efficient and specific than mineral or inorganic catalysts. Most enzymes catalyze only one reaction. It is conservatively estimated that the living cell contains 1,700 enzymes catalyzing as many different chemical reactions. A typical chemical make-up for an enzyme would be around twelve different **Amino Acids** with a molecular weight of 30,000 corresponding to 150 peptide bonds holding the amino-acid units in place. This corresponds to 150 factorial different possible arrangements of amino acids. It should also be noted that due to enzyme specificity one displaced amino-acid unit usually renders the original enzyme useless or at least greatly inhibits its biological activity.

Escape Velocity: The velocity which a gas molecule (or any other body) must acquire before it can escape from the gravitational influence of the earth and go into space.

Fatty Acid: Weakly acidic organic compounds of carbon, hydrogen, and oxygen which are essential to the formation of lipids (fats). They correspond to the general structure $CH_3(CH_2)_n COOH$ where n is between eight and eighteen.

Gene: A unit of heredity which provides the genetic code for the synthesis of **Enzymes**, which in turn are responsible for changes at the morphological level. The **Heterocyclic Bases** constitute a genetic alphabet of four letters on DNA or RNA. All genetic information appears to be contained within different code arrangements of the **Heterocyclic Bases** in DNA and RNA.

Genome: An organism's total gene pool.

Geocentric: A concept which maintained that the earth was the center of the universe.

Glutamic Acid: See **Amino Acid.**

Glycine: See **Amino Acid.**

Guanine: See **Heterocyclic Base.**

Heterocyclic Base: An organic structure containing one or more nitrogen atoms among carbon atoms in the cyclic arrangement. **Heterocyclic Bases** are either **Purines** or **Pyrimidines** and are essential to the formation of **Ribonucleic Acid (RNA)** and **Deoxyribonucleic Acid (DNA)**. See Figure 21 for the structures of the common heterocyclic bases.

Hetero-polymerization: The formation of a **Polymer** from two or more different **Monomers**. Proteins are hetero-polymers of the **Amino Acids**. Also see **Homo-polymerization**.

Homo-polymerization: The formation of a **Polymer** from a single **Monomer**. Starch and glycogen are homo-polymers of glucose. Also see **Hetero-polymerization**.

Lysosome: An interesting organelle that contains digestive enzymes that break down large molecules such as fats, proteins, and nucleic acids.

Mitochondria: The "power plant" of the cell. It is here that the oxidation of cellular foodstuffs mainly occurs.

Monomer: Individual molecular units which unite with one another to form very large molecules called **Polymers**.

Monosaccharides: Sugar molecules which contain only one sugar unit. Glucose, ribose, and deoxyribose are monosaccharides.

Natural Selection: The theory that molecules or living things combine to produce resultant species which compete for survival. Natural selection and mutation are used by the mechanistic materialist to explain the origin of life and its subsequent evolution.

Nucleus: The nucleus is the "computer center" of the cell. It is here that DNA and messenger RNA synthesis occurs. The RNA then moves to the **Cytoplasm** where it directs **Protein** synthesis on the **Ribosomes**.

Nucleolus: A body rich in RNA that appears to possibly be an active center of protein and RNA synthesis.

Nucleotides: An organic molecule containing a **Heterocyclic Base** bonded to either **Ribose** or **Deoxyribose** and a phosphate residue. The base combined to the sugar without the phosphate is called a nucleoside. See Figure 20 for the structure and composition of a typical nucleotide.

Panspermia: The theory which holds that germs of life dropped to earth, a suitable host for life, from interplanetary space in the form of viable spores or microorganisms. Most authorities hold that this theory is unlikely. Even if it is true, it begs the real question of the origin of life.

Pentose: A five-carbon atom sugar, usually **Ribose** or **Deoxyribose**.

Peptide: Any molecule formed by bonding an -NH$_2$ group of one amino acid with the -COOH group of another amino acid through the loss of a molecule of water. The resulting bond is called a peptide bond. **A Protein is a Polypeptide.** See Figure 17.

Photosynthesis: A chemical process by which plants, with the aid of

Chlorophyll, incorporate carbon dioxide from the atmosphere into the synthesis of carbohydrates.

$$n(CO_2 + H_2O) \xrightarrow{light} n(CH_2O) + nO_2$$

Plastids: A membrane-surrounded organelle peculiar to higher plant cells which have the property of self-replication.

Polymers: A large, high molecular weight molecule formed by the linear bonding of a number of fundamental units called monomers. In some polymers, such as cellulose, all monomers are the same; namely, glucose in the case of cellulose. In other polymers, such as **Proteins** and **Nucleic Acids**, the monomers are different, such as the twenty common **Amino Acids** for **Proteins**, and as many as thirteen different **Nucleotides** for the **Nucleic Acids**. However, only five of the thirteen **Nucleotides** are commonly found in nature.

Polymerization: The process by which monomers are converted into **Polymers**. In biochemical processes this reaction is catalyzed by specific enzymes. Most mechanists recognize the polymerization of **Amino Acids** into suitable **Proteins** and the conversion of **Nucleotides** into suitable **Polynucleotides** as being a formidable step in the evolution of a living thing.

Polynucleotides: **Polymers of Nucleotides. Ribonucleic Acid (RNA)** and **Deoxyribonucleic Acid (DNA)** are polynucleotides.

Polysaccharides: Very large molecules which result from the **Polymerization** of many simple sugar molecules. Cellulose is a structural polysaccharide, whereas amylose is a nutrient polysaccharide.

Porphyrins: A compound essential to the biosynthesis of **Chlorophyll**, hemoglobin, and the cytochromes, the latter being essential to respiration. It consists of a tetrapyrrole compound called porphin substituted at eight positions and a central metal ion; magnesium for chlorophyll and iron for hemoglobin and the cytochromes.

Pre-Biotic: Before the existence of life on earth.

Primordial: The state of the earth and the earth's atmosphere immediately or shortly after its formation.

Protein: A **Polypeptide Polymer** of some twenty **Amino Acids** with most proteins containing all twenty. A relatively simple protein would contain twelve different **Amino Acids**, molecular weight 34,000 with 288 **Peptide** bonds. **Enzymes**, which are proteins, must have specific structures in order to function properly as biological catalysts. There is no reason to assume that this is not true for **Pre-Biotic Enzymes** as well.

Proteinoid: A high molecular weight **Polymer** formed by S. W. Fox by heating mixtures of **Amino Acids** containing high concentrations of **Aspartic** and **Glutamic Acids.** These **Polymers** have some properties of **Proteins,** have some catalytic activity, and some nutritional value.

Purine: See Heterocyclic **Base.**

Pyrimidine: See Heterocyclic **Base.**

Ribonucleic Acid (RNA):   A single-stranded polynucleotide similar to Deoxyribonucleic Acid (DNA) except that ribonucleic acid (RNA) contains the sugar **Ribose** instead of **Deoxyribose** and the **Heterocyclic Base Uracil** instead of **Thymine.**

Ribose: A five-carbon atom sugar molecule that is essential to the formation of the **Polynucleotide Ribonucleic Acid (RNA).** See **Deoxyribose.**

Ribosomes: Bodies in the **Cytoplasm** consisting of **RNA** and **Protein** which are sites of active protein synthesis.

Serine: See **Amino Acid.**

Spontaneous Generation of Life: The hypothesis that life developed from nonliving matter freely and without assistance from any force independent of matter itself.

Tetrose: A four-carbon atom sugar.

Thymine: See **Heterocyclic Base.**

Triose: A three-carbon atom sugar.

Uracil: See **Heterocyclic Base.**

Vacuole: An air space.

Viruses: These are disease-causing particles which are much simpler than bacteria, which can multiply only inside a host cell. Many think that viruses may have bridged the gap between the living and the nonliving. They consist of **DNA** and/or **RNA** surrounded by a **Protein** coat. Virus particles discard the protein coat outside a host cell, but once inside the cell they multiply rapidly and produce new protein coats as they consume the **Nucleotides** and **Amino Acids** of the host cell. The viral **RNA/DNA** and protein coats reassemble into mature viruses and are released as the cell wall of the host cell collapses.